AF228274

STOMP

PEANUTS

Every Sunday

1956 – 1960

by Charles M. Schulz

FANTAGRAPHICS BOOKS, INC.

PEANUTS EVERY SUNDAY: 1956–1960 by Charles M. Schulz

FANTAGRAPHICS BOOKS

Editor: Gary Groth
Designer: Jacob Covey
Production: Paul Baresh
Color Production: Joanne Bagge
Associate Publisher: Eric Reynolds
Publisher: Gary Groth

Special thanks to Jeannie Schulz, without whom this project would not have come to fruition. Thanks to Charles M. Schulz Creative Associates, especially Paige Braddock.

Peanuts Every Sunday: 1956–1960 (Volume 2) is copyright © 2014 Peanuts Worldwide, LLC. The foreword is © 2014 Chuck Klosterman. All rights reserved. Permission to duplicate materials from *Peanuts* comic strips must be obtained from Peanuts Worldwide, LLC. Permission to quote or reproduce for reviews and notices must be obtained from the respective copyright holders. Peanuts Worldwide, LLC's *Peanuts*® website may be accessed at www.snoopy.com.

Fantagraphics Books, 7563 Lake City Way NE, Seattle, WA 98115, USA. For a free full-color catalog of comics, call 1-800-657-1100. Our books may be viewed on our website at www.fantagraphics.com.

ISBN: 978-1-60699-794-9
First printing: November 2014
Printed in China

Special thanks to: Philip Nel, Jason Aaron Wong, Randall Bethune, Big Planet Comics, Black Hook Press of Japan, Nick Capetillo, Kevin Czapiewski, John DiBello, Juan Manuel Domínguez, Andy Koopmans, Mathieu Doublet, Dan Evans III, Thomas Eykemans, Scott Fritsch-Hammes, Coco and Eddie Gorodetsky, Karen Green, Ted Haycraft, Eduardo Takeo "Lizarkeo" Igarashi, Nevdon Jamgochian, Vanessa Palacios, Kurt Sayenga, Anne Lise Rostgaard Schmidt, Christian Schremser, Secret Headquarters, Paul van Dijken, Mungo van Krimpen-Hall, and Thomas Zimmermann.

"I don't know what percentage of me would be Charlie Brown — certainly some. I'm a little bit of all the characters because that's what I draw. I used to be more Lucy than I am now, but I'm not much any more — I've learned to temper my sarcastic remarks. The strip is very personal and all the things in the strip are things that I think about."

— Charles Schulz, 1987

Resistance is Futile (Especially with Footballs)

Chuck Klosterman

It's difficult to write objectively about Charlie Brown. It always feels like I'm writing about myself.

This, I realize, is no accident.

I know that Charlie Brown is the type of character consciously designed to make average people feel like they're looking at an image of themselves. If you can't empathize with Charlie Brown, you likely lack an ability to empathize with any fictional character. Here is a boy continually humiliated for desiring nothing more than normalcy — the opportunity to kick a football, the aptitude to fly a kite, the freedom to walk down the sidewalk without having an acquaintance compare his skull to a block of lumber. He wants glory, but not an excessive amount (one baseball victory would be more than enough). He has the coolest dog in town, but that often plays to his disadvantage. He's an eight-year-old who needs a psychiatrist, and he has to pay the bill himself (only five cents, but still). Charlie Brown knows his life is a contradictory struggle, and sometimes his only option is to lie in a dark room, alone with his thoughts. He will never win. Yet here's the paradox: Charlie Brown is still happy. He still has friends. He still gets excited about all the things that are destined to fail.

Very often, young Americans are simultaneously pessimistic about the world and optimistic about themselves — they assume everyone's future is bleak, except (somehow) their own. Charlie Brown is the opposite. He knows *he's* doomed, but that doesn't stop him from trying anything and everything. It's the quality that makes him so infinitely likeable: he does not see the world as cruel. He believes the world is good, even if everything that's ever happened in his life suggests otherwise. All he wants are the things everyone else seems to get without trying. He aspires to be average, which — for him — is an impossible dream.

I suppose nobody feels this way all the time. But everybody feels this way some of the time.

Charles M. Schulz died on February 12, 2000. The final *Peanuts* strip ran the very next day, a coincidence noted by virtually everyone who cared about the man and his work. In the years since his passing, I've noticed a curious trend: for whatever reason, it has become popular to assert that the spiritual center of the *Peanuts* universe is not Charlie Brown. The modern answer to that question is Snoopy: dynamic, indefatigable, and hyper-imaginative. Perception has drifted toward what the public prefers to celebrate. It's a little like what happened on the TV show *Happy Days*: a sitcom originally focused on awkward Richie Cunningham evolved into a vehicle for the super-coolness of Fonzie. Obviously, this type of paradigm shift is no crime against humanity, and I love Snoopy almost as much as his owner (he's a wonderful dancer, and he might be my all-time favorite novelist). But Snoopy is not the emotional vortex of *Peanuts*. That's simply wrong. The linchpin to *Peanuts* will always be Charlie Brown. It can be no one else. And this is because Charlie Brown effortlessly embodies what *Peanuts* truly is: an introduction to adult problems, explained by children.

The probable (read: inevitable) death of daily newspapers will yield a lot of collateral damage, some of which will matter more than others. I don't know where the gradual disappearance of the Sunday comics falls on this continuum, or even if it belongs at all; I assume something else will replace its role in the culture, and the notion of bemoaning such a loss will eventually be categorized as nostalgia for a period where the media was controlled by dinosaurs who refused to accept that the purpose of every news story was to provide random people the opportunity to publicly comment on how they felt about it.

But I will miss the Sunday comics. As a kid, I loved the idea that there was at least one section of the newspaper directly targeted at my brain; as an adult, it was reassuring to read something that was still the exact same product I remembered from the past. It was static in the best possible way. Like most people, I moved through various adolescent phases where different strips temporarily became my favorite: *Garfield* in fifth grade, *The Far Side* throughout high school, *Calvin and Hobbes* as a college boozehound. But I always considered *Peanuts* the most "important" comic strip, and the one that all other strips were measured against. The fact that *Peanuts* was the very first strip on the top of the Sunday comics' front page verified this subjective belief; if comics were rock bands, it seemed obvious that *Peanuts* was the Beatles.

The strips in this collection stretch from 1956 to 1960. This was a transitional period for *Peanuts* — the characters no longer have the generic, unsophisticated appearance seen in the early *Li'l Folks* era, but their fantasies and dialogue rarely skew as surreal as they will become throughout the mid-'60s and beyond. Snoopy "talks," but not in the way we're accustomed to (his concerns tend to be more traditionally dog-like), and his jowls and his gut look a little thin. Linus Van Pelt — still noticeably younger than all the other kids in '57 — eventually becomes interchangeable with his slightly older peers (and Schulz was clearly enamored with Linus during this five-year stretch, as he stars in a majority of the offerings, most notably in a three-week serial where he worries about performing at the Christmas program). Around 1959, we meet Sally Brown for the first time (still an infant).

But the most critical evolution revolves around the persona of Charlie Brown himself. It is during this three-year stretch that he becomes "The Charlie Browniest." Throughout the mid-'50s, Charlie Brown was still confident. On page 13, we see a boy who believes his snow fort is an architectural masterwork; on page 31, Charlie Brown violently punishes the kite he cannot fly. He's not arrogant, but he is self-assured. He's almost a smart aleck. Yet, by the inception of the '60s, this is over. From 1960 onward, Charlie Brown is the person we all recognize from all those various television specials: the unironic loser with a limitless heart, who is endlessly hammered for caring too much.

"Nobody likes me," Charlie Brown says as he stares into space. "All it would take to make me happy is have someone say he likes me."

When Lucy overhears this gut-wrenching lament, she's immediately incredulous. "Do you mean to tell me that someone has it within his or her power to make you happy merely by doing such a simple thing?"

Charlie assures her that — yes — this simple act is all it would take. In fact, it almost wouldn't matter if the sentiment weren't true. He just wants to know how it feels to be liked. But even this is still too much to ask for.

"I can't do it," Lucy replies, and then she walks away.

And this, it seems, is the joke.

One of the most common assumptions about *Peanuts* is that Charlie Brown and Charles M. Schulz are the same person, and that we are able to see the personality of

Schulz by studying the personality of Charlie Brown. Certainly, some similarities are undeniable (both their fathers are barbers). But I don't think this perception is totally accurate. The reflection is not as straightforward as it seems. I think that the primordial *Li'l Folks* version of Charlie Brown — the little guy from the '40s — was Schulz crafting a fictional version of his literal childhood. It was, essentially, who Schulz once was. But the model of Charlie Brown we recognize and love so much more — the model re-invented here, at the end of the '50s — was Schulz crafting a version of how he *felt*, both in his memory and in the present tense. It was the construct of an adult, suffering through problems only an adult can conceive and recognize. It was also (perhaps) a depiction of how he *wanted* to feel: Schulz the man was rumored to be a maniacal grudge holder, unwilling to forget any slight or embarrassment ever levied against him. His creative boyhood doppelganger is the opposite; Charlie Brown could always wipe the slate clean. And that makes a profound difference, both for the character and everyone else.

"It's depressing to realize that you're so insignificant you haven't got a chance ever to become president," Charlie Brown tells Lucy on page 89. "It wouldn't be so bad if I thought I had *some* chance."

Like so much of the classic *Peanuts* banter, he makes these remarks apropos of nothing — it's just something he seems to be worrying about, for no clear reason. Lucy, of course, obliterates him for voicing this trepidation, mocking him with a tsunami of faint praise, almost as if he had somehow claimed he was destined for political greatness. Now, is her response amusing? I suppose it's a little amusing. But it's mostly dark (and entirely true). At the age of eight, Charlie Brown is considering a reality that most people don't confront until much later: the realization that life is limited. It's not that he desperately wants to become Dwight D. Eisenhower; it's the simple recognition that this couldn't happen even if he did. He's confronting the central myth of childhood, which is that anyone can be anything. Charlie Brown represents the downside of adult consciousness. And what does Lucy represent? Lucy represents the world itself. Lucy responds the way society always responds to any sudden insight of existential despair: *How did you not know this already*? It doesn't matter how many times this had happened before. It will never stop happening, to Charlie Brown or to anyone else. Like I said — Charlie Brown knows he's doomed. He absolutely, irrefutably knows it. But part of his mind always thinks, "Maybe not this time, though. Maybe I'm wrong."

That glimmer of hope is his true Achilles' heel. It's also the quality that makes him so deeply good and imminently relatable. The joke is not that Charlie Brown is hopeless. The joke is that Charlie Brown *knows* he's hopeless, but he doesn't trust the infallibility of his own insecurity. If he's always wrong about everything, perhaps he's wrong about this. When he mentions the impossibility of his own presidential fantasy, there's a vague sense that he wants Lucy to tell him he's mistaken. And at first (of course), Lucy does exactly that. She says "maybe." And then (of course) she does what she always does. She reminds Charlie Brown that he is Charlie Brown. Which is how I suspect Charles M. Schulz often felt about himself, up until the very end: "No matter what I do or what I try, I'm always going to be myself."

In this volume, there are four strips where Charlie Brown tries to kick a football. Unless you're a yet-to-be-conceived archaeologist reading this book 1,000 years in the future, the outcome of these attempts will not surprise you. Two of theses strips (released roughly a year apart) are so similar they superficially suggest a lack of imagination. In one, Charlie Brown expresses his belief that people have the ability to change and deserve the opportunity to do so (and then he breaks his back); in the other, Lucy compliments his faith in human nature (moments after his back has been broken). This is the reassuring, hyper-eternal, death-and-taxes aspect to *Peanuts;* the children don't grow up and the episodes don't change. That pigskin's omnipresent unkickability is the Sisyphean symbol for everything in Charlie Brown's life and the pivotal metaphor behind why he matters so much to so many people. It is the apex of his failures. But failing is not what makes Charlie Brown my fictional friend and my personal protagonist. It is his reasoning for placing himself in a position where failure is inevitable.

"I must be out of my mind," he says to himself. "But I can't resist kicking footballs." He can't resist kicking footballs. Even though he never, ever does. He still can't resist. Charlie Brown will always be himself.

Chuck Klosterman is the author of six nonfiction books (including Sex, Drugs, and Cocoa Puffs *and* I Wear the Black Hat*) and two novels (*Downtown Owl *and* The Visible Man*). He has also written for* GQ, Esquire, Spin, The Washington Post, The Guardian, The Believer, *and* The A.V. Club. *He currently covers sports and popular culture for ESPN and serves as "The Ethicist" for the* New York Times Magazine.

I ADMIRE YOU, CHARLIE BROWN... YOU HAVE SUCH FAITH IN HUMAN NATURE..

PEANUTS

Every Sunday

1956 – 1960

HEY, CHARLIE BROWN! I THOUGHT WE WERE GONNA MAKE A SNOWMAN?!
PEANUTS
by
CHARLES M. SCHULZ
I CHANGED MY MIND.. IT'S TOO COLD...

NO MATTER HOW MUCH I WEAR, I STILL GET COLD.. I MUST HAVE THIN BLOOD...

WHUMP!

?

GOOD GRIEF! I'VE GOT SO MANY CLOTHES ON, I CAN'T MOVE! **I CAN'T GET UP!**

WHEW IT'S NO USE... I'M DOOMED... I'LL NEVER GET HOME.. I'LL HAVE TO LIE HERE UNTIL I FREEZE TO DEATH....

?
?
THIS IS THE MOST EMBARRASSING THING THAT'S EVER HAPPENED TO ME!
1-1
SCHULZ

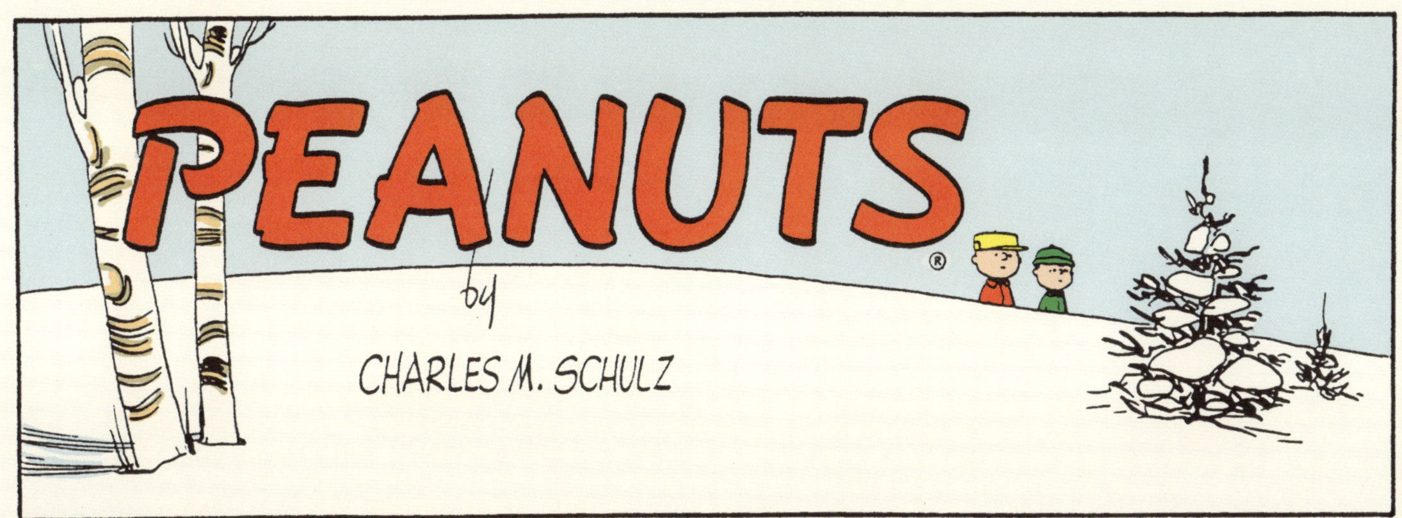
PEANUTS
by
CHARLES M. SCHULZ

THIS LOOKS LIKE A GOOD SPOT..

YOU BUILD YOUR SNOW FORT 'WAY OVER THERE LINUS, AND I'LL BUILD MINE HERE..

LET ME KNOW WHEN YOU'RE READY, AND WE'LL HAVE A BIG BATTLE..

AH! AN IMPREGNABLE FORTRESS OF SNOW!

THAT POOR LITTLE KID WILL BE SICK WITH JEALOUSY WHEN HE SEES WHAT I'VE BUILT...

I'M NOT READY..
1-8
SCHULZ

PEANUTS
by
CHARLES M. SCHULZ
?

CHOMP CHOMP
CHOMP CHOMP
COOKIES!

CHOMP
CHOMP

CHOMP
CHOMP
CHOMP
!

CHOMP
CHOMP

THUD!

CHOMP CHOMP
CHOMP CHOMP
1-15
SCHULZ

PEANUTS
by SCHULZ
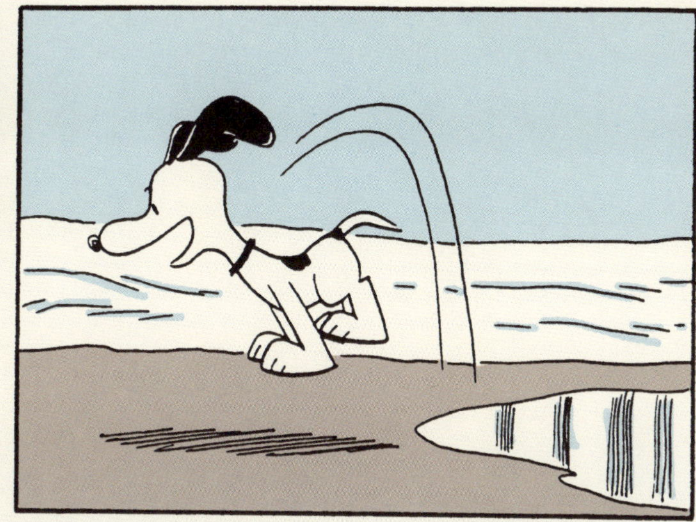

?

!

THAT'S THE WAY IT GOES...
1-22
SCHULZ

PEANUTS
by
CHARLES M. SCHULZ

?

OH, GOOD GRIEF!

WHAM

SCHULZ 1-29
WHEN? WHEN? WHEN? WHEN? WHEN WILL I EVER LEARN?

PEANUTS
by
CHARLES M. SCHULZ
WHERE'S MY BLANKET? I CAN'T GO TO BED WITHOUT MY BLANKET...

GIMME THAT BLANKET!

GIMME IT, I SAY!

WHEW

BANG!
2-5
SCHULZ

PEANUTS®
by
CHARLES M. SCHULZ

?

2-12
SCHULZ

PEANUTS
by
CHARLES M. SCHULZ
RATS!

LUCY, WILL YOU WIND MY TRAIN FOR ME?

THANK YOU!
WHIRR

WHIRRRRRRR

RRRRRRRR

SCHULZ 2-19
RRRRRRRRRRR

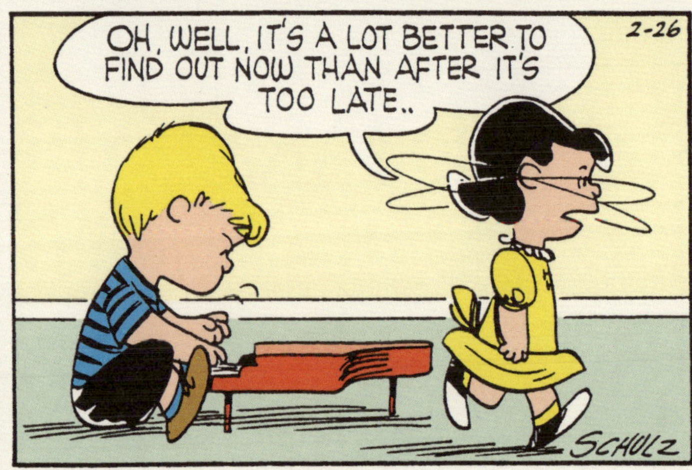

 FEBRUARY 26, 1956

PEANUTS
by
CHARLES M. SCHULZ
I OUGHT TO KNOW... I SAW IT ON TELEVISION!

YOU WOULDN'T KNOW IF YOU SAW IT IN REAL LIFE!

IT WAS ROBIN HOOD!

IT WAS NOT! IT WAS WILLIAM TELL!! AND I'M GOING TO PROVE IT TO YOU!!!

SEE? IT SAYS SO RIGHT HERE IN THIS BOOK! SEE?

WHAT DO YOU THINK OF THAT, SMARTY? HUH? SMARTY, SMARTY, SMARTY !!

TWANG!
SCHULZ
3-4

MARCH 4, 1956

PEANUTS
by
CHARLES M.
SCHULZ
YOU WEREN'T USING THEM!
I DON'T CARE! I WANT THEM NOW!

WELL, YOU'RE NOT GONNA GET 'EM!

MOMMY! LINUS WON'T GIVE ME MY SCISSORS!

LINUS! GIVE THEM BACK...THEY BELONG TO YOUR SISTER, YOU KNOW..BESIDES, YOU MIGHT CUT YOURSELF...

NYAAHH!
!
SMARTY SMARTY SMARTY

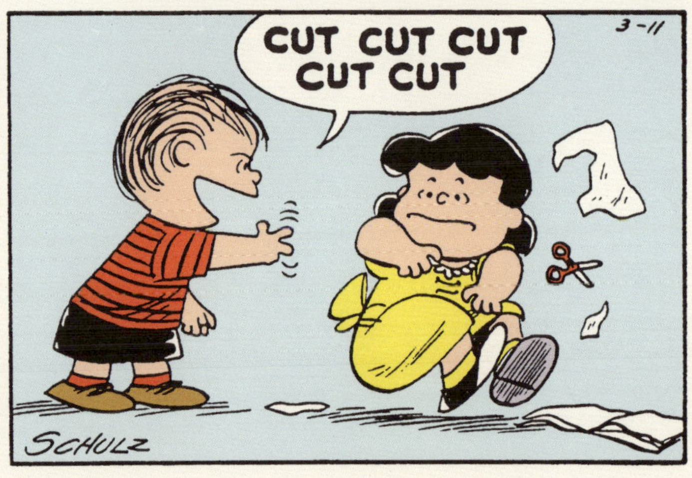
3-11
CUT CUT CUT CUT CUT
SCHULZ

PEANUTS
by
CHARLES M. SCHULZ
SOMETIMES I THINK I'D LIKE TO BE ALMOST ANYTHING BUT A DOG..

BIRDS ARE THE PEOPLE I ENVY THE MOST...

BOY! THERE'S THE LIFE!

SIGH!

?

3-18
SCHULZ

PEANUTS
MARCH 1956
JANUARY, FEBRUARY, MARCH...

ONE TWO, THREE, FOUR, FIVE!

GOOD GRIEF! SPRING BEGAN FIVE DAYS AGO!

I GOTTA CALL SCHROEDER...I'LL BET HE DOESN'T EVEN KNOW IT...

WADDYA MEAN, Y'DON'T CARE WHAT THE CALENDAR SAYS?!

BY GOLLY, I SURE CARE WHAT THE CALENDAR SAYS!

C'MON! LET'S PLAY BALL!!
3-25
SCHULZ

PEANUTS
NOTICE ANYTHING PECULIAR?
NOT A THING!
I WAS AFRAID OF THAT...
IT'S STARTING TO RAIN, CHARLIE BROWN...
WHO CARES? A LITTLE RAIN NEVER HURT ANYBODY!
Y'GOTTA ADMIRE THAT CHARLIE BROWN..HE MAY BE AN IDIOT, BUT Y'GOTTA ADMIRE HIM..
YOU'RE SURE YOU DON'T WANNA GO HOME?
OF COURSE, I'M SURE!!
JUST THOUGHT I'D ASK, THAT'S ALL..NO HARM IN JUST ASKING
YOU KNOW WHAT, CHARLIE BROWN?
WHAT?!
I DON'T THINK THE OTHER TEAM IS GOING TO SHOW UP..
SCHULZ

GET 'WAY OUT, LINUS...
PEANUTS
CHARLES M. SCHULZ

'WAY OUT!

GOOD GRIEF!
4-8
SCHULZ

 APRIL 8, 1956

PEANUTS
by
CHARLES M. SCHULZ
LET'S GET OUT HERE IN THE OPEN WHERE WE WON'T HURT ANYBODY...
?

I GUESS THIS IS ALL RIGHT...

OKAY, LUCY...NOW TOSS THE RECORD IN THE AIR...

BANG!

IS THERE A HOLE IN THE CENTER?
OF COURSE..

FASTEST GUN IN THE WEST!
4-15
SCHULZ

PEANUTS
by
CHARLES M. SCHULZ

RATS..
SNAP!

RATS!
SNAP!

RATS!!
SNAP!

SIGH...

I JUST LEARNED SOMETHING...
OH?

NO MATTER HOW HARD YOU TRY, YOU CAN'T BEND A CRACKER!
4-22
SCHULZ

PEANUTS
by
CHARLES M. SCHULZ
HOW CAN I PRACTICE WITH YOU LEANING ON THE PIANO ALL THE TIME?!

GOOD GRIEF! YOU SURE ARE A NUISANCE!

WHY CAN'T YOU BE MORE FRIENDLY TOWARD ME, SCHROEDER?

I'M ALWAYS FRIENDLY TOWARD YOU...I TRY TO BE WHAT YOU WANT ME TO BE...
!

AND YET, YOU NEVER EVEN SMILE AT ME...

COULDN'T YOU AT LEAST GIVE ME A LITTLE SMILE?

SIGH I'LL PROBABLY NEVER GET MARRIED...
4-29
SCHULZ

PEANUTS
by CHARLES M. SCHULZ
FOOEY!
'FOOEY' IS RIGHT!
FLIP

SHE'S HOPELESS, CHARLIE BROWN..

WHY DO WE HAVE TO LET HER PLAY ?!

DON'T WORRY ABOUT IT... SHE'LL GET DISCOURAGED RIGHT AWAY, AND GO HOME..
!
BLIP!

RATS!
SEE? SHE'S DISCOURAGED ALREADY...NOW SHE WON'T BOTHER US ANY MORE..

OH, NO!
WHAT'S THE MATTER?

WHAM!

5-6
"SEE? SHE'S DISCOURAGED ALREADY...NOW SHE WON'T BOTHER US ANY MORE.."
SCHULZ

PEANUTS
BY
CHARLES M. SCHULZ

THAT STUPID KITE WENT DOWN AGAIN!

KITES DRIVE ME CRAZY!

I'VE NEVER SEEN ONE YET THAT DIDN'T GET ITSELF ALL TANGLED UP IN EVERYTHING.. EXCUSE ME...
?

I WONDER WHERE THAT FOOL THING WENT DOWN?

HOW I HATE KITES!! I'LL NEVER BUY ANOTHER ONE AS LONG AS I LIVE!!!

EXCUSE ME...

I HATE EVERY BONE IN THAT KITE'S BODY!

GOOD GRIEF!! WHAT A MESS!

SO THAT'S WHERE YOU CAME DOWN, EH? GOOD!

BURN, YOU MONSTER!!
5-13
SCHULZ

PEANUTS
by
CHARLES M. SCHULZ

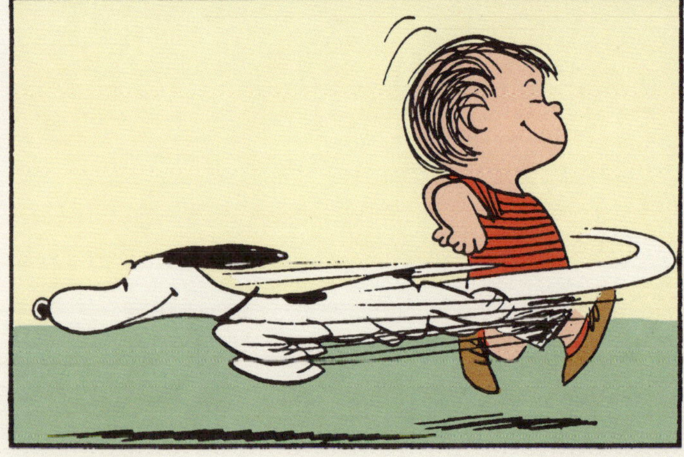

5-20
SCHULZ

PEANUTS
by
CHARLES M. SCHULZ

THIS IS
RETRIEVING?
5-27
SCHULZ

PEANUTS®
by
CHARLES M. SCHULZ

LINUS IS ALWAYS WRITING SOMETHING IN THE AIR..

SOMETIMES HE WRITES, SOMETIMES HE DRAWS, SOMETIMES HE JUST SKETCHES...

?

EVERY NOW AND THEN HE LIKES TO DO A **MURAL**!
SCHULZ
6-3

PEANUTS
by CHARLES M. SCHULZ
I WISH THAT
I LOOKED
REAL TOUGH..

I WONDER WHAT SOME DOGS DO TO MAKE THEMSELVES LOOK TOUGH?

FANGS!

BY GOLLY, THAT'S WHAT YOU HAVE TO HAVE IF YOU'RE GOING TO SCARE PEOPLE!

FANGS AND A REAL FIERCE EXPRESSION

HERE COMES THAT STUPID LINUS AND HIS EQUALLY STUPID SISTER.. I'LL SHOW 'EM THE OL' FANGS, AND SCARE THE DAYLIGHTS OUT OF THEM!

SIGH
6-10
SCHULZ

OH, GOOD GRIEF! NOT **AGAIN**!
PEANUTS
by
CHARLES M. SCHULZ

I CAN'T STAND IT..

KITE CAUGHT IN THE SAME TREE AGAIN, EH, CHARLIE BROWN?

WHY DON'T YOU LET ME **YELL** AT IT? WILL YOU LET ME YELL AT IT FOR YOU, CHARLIE BROWN?

I DON'T CARE **WHAT** YOU DO! YOU CAN YELL AT IT 'TIL YOUR **HEAD** FALLS OFF AS FAR AS **I'M** CONCERNED...
GOOD

!

YOU STUPID KITE! COME DOWN OUT OF THAT TREE!!!

SCHULZ
6-17

 JUNE 17, 1956

OH, NO! LOOK WHO'S COMING...
"PIG-PEN," THE HUMAN DUST-BOWL!
PEANUTS
by
CHARLES M. SCHULZ

GOOD MORNING, VIOLET...'MORNING, CHARLIE BROWN..

"PIG-PEN" IS THE ONLY PERSON I KNOW WHO CAN RAISE A CLOUD OF DUST ON A CLEAN SIDEWALK!
AAK!! KOFF! KOFF!

Z

?
!

GOOD GRIEF! I THOUGHT I HAD BEEN BURIED ALIVE!
6-24
SCHULZ

PEANUTS
CHARLES M. SCHULZ
?

EASY NOW....

GENTLY.... GENTLY....

KLUNK!
GULP!

YOU'RE THE ONLY PERSON I KNOW WHO CAN BE DEFT AND CLUMSY AT THE SAME TIME!
7-1
SCHULZ

PEANUTS
by
CHARLES M. SCHULZ
DISGRACEFUL!
OH, GO AWAY!

COMPLETELY DISGRACEFUL!

YOU AND THAT STUPID BLANKET! ARE YOU GONNA CARRY THAT THING AROUND THE REST OF YOUR LIFE?

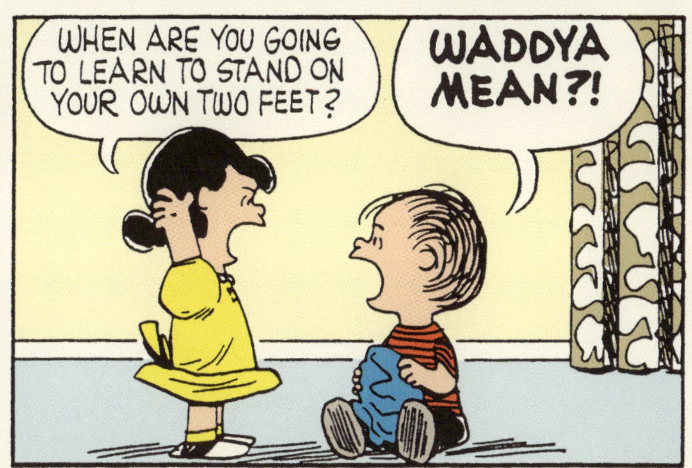
WHEN ARE YOU GOING TO LEARN TO STAND ON YOUR OWN TWO FEET?
WADDYA MEAN?!

I'VE GOT JUST AS MUCH WILL POWER AS ANYONE ELSE! SEE? I DON'T NEED THIS BLANKET! I CAN THROW IT AWAY ANYTIME I WANT TO! ANYTIME!

GOOD GRIEF!

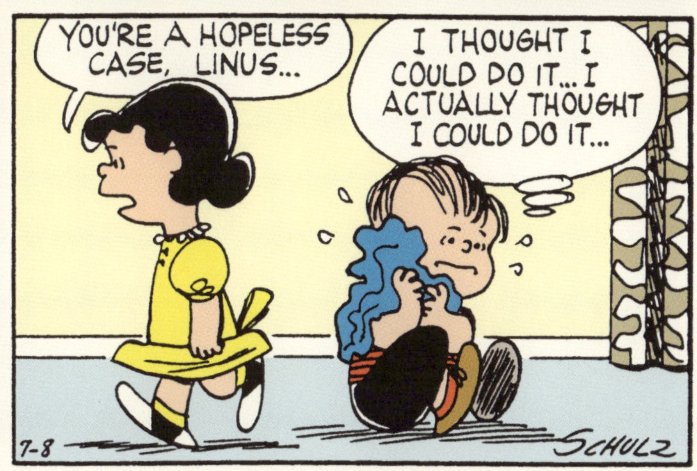
YOU'RE A HOPELESS CASE, LINUS...
I THOUGHT I COULD DO IT... I ACTUALLY THOUGHT I COULD DO IT...
7-8
SCHULZ

PEANUTS®
by
CHARLES M. SCHULZ
C'MON! HIT ONE OUT HERE!

PLUCK

GREATEST CATCH I'VE EVER SEEN!
7-15
SCHULZ

PEANUTS
by
CHARLES M. SCHULZ

!

"RAIN, RAIN, GO AWAY.. COME AGAIN SOME **OTHER** DAY !!"

I **SAID** "RAIN, RAIN, GO AWAY.. COME AGAIN SOME **OTHER** DAY !!!"

7-22

YOU'RE NOT LISTENING!
SCHULZ

PEANUTS
by
CHARLES M. SCHULZ
LOOK AT THAT SMUG EXPRESSION...

HA! I GOT IT!

I'LL TEACH YOU TO BE SO SMUG! I'M GONNA TEAR THIS BLANKET TO SHREDS!

I'M GONNA TEAR IT INTO A **MILLION** PIECES!!

THERE! NOW WHAT ARE YOU GOING TO DO, SMARTY?

THAT WASN'T MY BLANKET... THAT WAS **YOURS**!

7-29
NO, NO, NO, NO, NO, NO!
SCHULZ

PEANUTS
by
CHARLES M. SCHULZ

I BEG YOUR PARDON...
?

THANK YOU, GIRLS..
SCHULZ
8 5

PEANUTS
by
CHARLES M. SCHULZ

I'VE NEVER BEEN SO TIRED IN ALL MY LIFE..

WHEW I CAN'T STOP YAWNING..

?
Z

WHAT'S THE BIG IDEA?!! GO LEAN ON SOMEBODY ELSE!

IF YOU'RE SO TIRED, WHY DON'T YOU GO HOME, AND GO TO BED?!

Z
?

GET AWAY FROM ME!

WHAT'S THE MATTER, SNOOPY? WON'T ANYONE LET YOU LEAN ON HIM?

WELL, C'MON..YOU CAN PUT YOUR HEAD ON ME...
SIGH

8-12
SCHULZ
RATS! NOW I'M WIDE AWAKE!

AUGUST 19, 1956

PEANUTS
by CHARLES M. SCHULZ

WHAT'S GOING ON HERE?

WHOOSH

ZOOM

I GUESS I KNEW I'D NEVER GET AWAY WITH IT.
8-26.
SCHULZ

SEPTEMBER 2, 1956

PEANUTS
by
CHARLES M. SCHULZ

?
I DON'T WANT TO WATCH THAT PROGRAM..I WANT TO WATCH THIS PROGRAM!
CLICK!

YAUGHH!

BANG! BANG! BANG! BANG! BANG! BANG!

Grrrowrr!

POW! POW! POW!

9-9
SIGH
SCHULZ

SEPTEMBER 16, 1956

PEANUTS
by
CHARLES M. SCHULZ
OKAY, MAC! STAY RIGHT WHERE YOU ARE!
!

PHOOEY!

I'M GOING TO GET THAT BLANKET AWAY FROM THAT STUPID KID IF IT KILLS ME!

I THINK I'LL USE THE OL' SURPRISE ATTACK, THE WAY MY WOLF ANCESTORS DID...

ZOOM!

CLOMP!

AAUGH!

GOOD GRIEF!
9-23
SCHULZ

PEANUTS
by
CHARLES M. SCHULZ

SCHROEDER, DO PIANO PLAYERS MAKE A LOT OF MONEY?

MONEY?

WHO CARES ABOUT MONEY?! THIS IS **ART**, YOU BLOCKHEAD!!

THIS IS GREAT MUSIC I'M PLAYING, AND PLAYING GREAT MUSIC IS AN **ART**!! DO YOU HEAR ME? **AN ART!**

ART! ART! ART! ART! ART!
WHAM
WHAM
WHAM
WHAM
WHAM

YOU FASCINATE ME!
9-30
SCHULZ

PEANUTS
by
CHARLES M. SCHULZ
CHOMP
CHOMP
CHOMP

CHOMP
CHOMP

HERE, SNOOPY.. YOU CAN HAVE THE REST..

'THE REST'... THAT'S THE WAY IT ALWAYS IS... I GET THE LEFT OVERS..

I SUPPOSE THERE ISN'T EVEN ANY HOT DOG LEFT IN THERE.. PROBABLY JUST THE ENDS OF THE BUN...

THEY ALWAYS ACT LIKE THEY'RE DOING YOU SUCH A BIG FAVOR, TOO... HUH... SOME FAVOR...

GULP!

10-7
IT'S FUNNY HOW MUCH CAN PASS THROUGH YOUR MIND BETWEEN THE TOSS AND THE GULP...
SCHULZ

PEANUTS
by
CHARLES M. SCHULZ
PHOOEY!

WHAT DO YOU MEAN, 'PHOOEY'?
JUST WHAT I SAID! PHOOEY!

FOR GOODNESS' SAKE, LINUS, STOP COMPLAINING!

WELL, GOOD GRIEF, HOW DOES IT LOOK TO HAVE TO HAVE MY SISTER TAG AFTER ME TO HELP ME HOLD ON TO A STUPID BALLOON?!

ALL RIGHT, I'LL TIE IT ON TO YOUR SHOELACE, AND YOU CAN TAKE CARE OF IT YOURSELF!
GOOD!

HEY, WAIT!

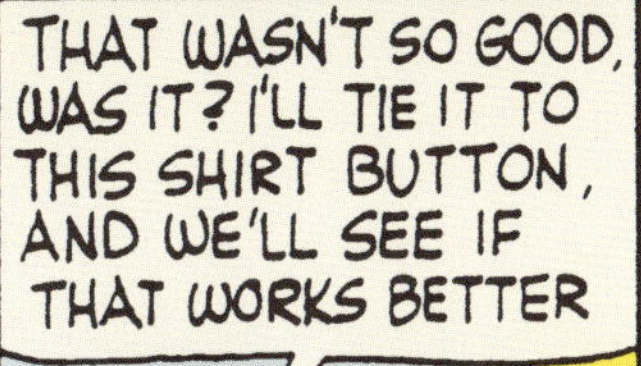
THAT WASN'T SO GOOD, WAS IT? I'LL TIE IT TO THIS SHIRT BUTTON, AND WE'LL SEE IF THAT WORKS BETTER

NOPE, I GUESS IT DOESN'T!

THIS TIME I'LL TIE IT TO YOUR COLLAR.. THAT SHOULD WORK..

WHEW! WHAT A STRUGGLE! I'M GLAD WE GOT THAT STRAIGHTENED OUT..
WHOOPS
10-14

DON'T SAY A WORD! JUST DON'T SAY ANYTHING!!
SCHULZ

PEANUTS
by
CHARLES M. SCHULZ

HERE, SNOOPY... CHASE THE BALL...

!

WHAM!

WHEW WHAT A BLOW!

HERE, KID

SCHULZ
10-21
THIS IS RETRIEVING?

PEANUTS
by
CHARLES M. SCHULZ

10-28
SIGH
SCHULZ

PEANUTS
by CHARLES M. SCHULZ
WAIT 'TIL I WIND IT UP..

THERE..NOW, LISTEN..

ISN'T THAT BEAUTIFUL?

THAT WAS 'ROCK-A-BYE, BABY.' I BROUGHT IT OVER JUST SO YOU COULD HEAR IT!
WELL! THAT WAS VERY NICE..

YOU SHOULD HAVE A MUSIC-BOX, SCHROEDER..

?

!
TOCCATA AND FUGUE in D MINOR BY BACH
11-4

I MIGHT HAVE KNOWN..
SCHULZ

PEANUTS
by
CHARLES M. SCHULZ
DISGRACEFUL!

DANCE! DANCE! DANCE!

THAT'S ALL YOU GUYS EVER THINK OF!!

IF YOU KEEP HANGING AROUND WITH THAT STUPID DOG, LINUS, YOU'LL END UP JUST AS WORTHLESS AS HE IS! YOU'LL BE A NOTHING!!

DO YOU HEAR ME? YOU'LL BE A **NOTHING**!!

FIVE HUNDRED YEARS FROM NOW, WHO'LL KNOW THE DIFFERENCE?!

SIGH YOUTH NEVER LISTENS..
11-11
SCHULZ

PEANUTS
by
CHARLES M. SCHULZ

?

!
!

WHEN YOU HAVE CLAUSTROPHOBIA, YOU LEARN TO WALK ON **TOP** OF THE WEEDS!
11-18
SCHULZ

NOVEMBER 25, 1956

PEANUTS
by
CHARLES M. SCHULZ

AAK

KOFF
KOFF
GASP
GASP
KOFF!

WHEW

YOU'RE THE ONLY PERSON I'VE EVER KNOWN WHO COULD CHOKE ON A SNOWFLAKE!
12-2
SCHULZ

PEANUTS

by

CHARLES M. SCHULZ

PEANUTS
by CHARLES M. SCHULZ
NO!
OH, COME ON, CHARLIE BROWN..

I'LL HOLD IT REAL STEADY...

NO!

PLEASE?

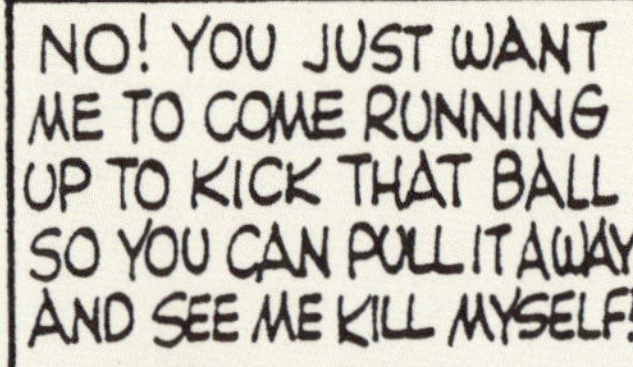
NO! YOU JUST WANT ME TO COME RUNNING UP TO KICK THAT BALL SO YOU CAN PULL IT AWAY AND SEE ME KILL MYSELF!

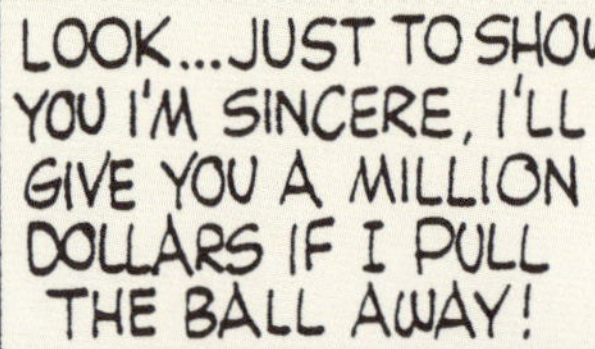
LOOK...JUST TO SHOW YOU I'M SINCERE, I'LL GIVE YOU A MILLION DOLLARS IF I PULL THE BALL AWAY!

IN FACT, I'LL GIVE YOU A **HUNDRED** MILLION DOLLARS!!

I MUST BE OUT OF MY MIND, BUT I CAN'T RESIST KICKING FOOTBALLS..

HA!

WHAM

HERE'S YOUR MONEY, CHARLIE BROWN!

HEE HEE HEE
HEE HEE HEE

I THINK I'LL JUST LIE HERE UNTIL THE FIRST SNOW COMES AND COVERS ME UP...
12-16
SCHULZ

PEANUTS
by
CHARLES M. SCHULZ

!

12-23
SCHULZ

PEANUTS
by
CHARLES M. SCHULZ
BEAUTIFUL!
BEAUTIFUL!

MMMMMMMMM

MMMMM

♪

?

!

12-30
SCHULZ
SIGH

JANUARY 6, 1957

PEANUTS
by
CHARLES M. SCHULZ
!

I FOUND THEM!

I FOUND MY MITTENS! I FOUND MY MITTENS!

WHERE'S THE PIE?
PIE? WHAT PIE?!
STORIES

I FOUND MY MITTENS! WHEN YOU FIND YOUR MITTENS, YOU'RE SUPPOSED TO GET SOME PIE!
STORIES

OH, DON'T BE SO STUPID!

MOTHER HASN'T MADE A PIE IN THREE WEEKS!

WHAT GOOD DOES IT DO TO FIND YOUR MITTENS IF YOU DON'T GET ANY PIE?
SCHULZ
1-13

PEANUTS
by
CHARLES M. SCHULZ

MY BLANKET IS IN THE DRYER..HOW LONG DO YOU THINK IT'LL TAKE TO GET DRY?

HOW IN THE WORLD SHOULD I KNOW?
I GOTTA HAVE THAT BLANKET..

SIGH
1-20

THIS IS A LONELY VIGIL...
SCHULZ

PEANUTS
by
CHARLES M. SCHULZ

?
POW!

!
WHAM!

?
POW!

I FEEL TORN BETWEEN THE DESIRE TO CREATE AND THE DESIRE TO DESTROY..
1-27
SCHULZ

PEANUTS®
by
CHARLES M. SCHULZ

2-3
SCHULZ

PEANUTS
by
CHARLES M. SCHULZ
CRUNCH

CHOMP
CHOMP
CHOMP

CRUNCH

CHOMP CHOMP
CHOMP

CHOMP CHOMP
CHOMP
2-10
SCHULZ

FEBRUARY 17, 1957

PEANUTS
by
CHARLES M. SCHULZ

SIGH

LUCY... HOW LONG BEFORE MY COWBOY PROGRAM COMES ON?

PRETTY SOON..

SAY, YOU WANNA TRY TO GUESS A SECRET?

DADDY'S GOING TO TAKE US SKATING?

NOPE!
GRAMPA'S COMING OVER?

NOPE!
MOM MADE SOME DOUGHNUTS?

NOPE!
WE'RE ALL GOING TO THE SHOW?

NOPE!
I'M GOING TO GET SOME NEW SHOES?

NOPE!
TOMORROW IS MY BIRTHDAY?

NOPE!
GEE...

I GIVE UP... WHAT'S THE SECRET?

YOU'VE JUST MISSED YOUR PROGRAM!
2-24
SCHULZ

PEANUTS
by
CHARLES M. SCHULZ
WHY CAN'T WE EVER WATCH WHAT I WANT TO WATCH?

WHY CAN'T WE? HUH? WHY CAN'T WE?

I'M TIRED OF ALWAYS HAVING TO WATCH YOUR PROGRAMS!

IN FACT, I THINK I'LL CHANGE THE CHANNEL RIGHT NOW!

I THINK I'LL WALK RIGHT OVER THERE, AND CHANGE THE CHANNEL...THAT'S JUST WHAT I'LL DO..I'LL WALK RIGHT OVER THERE, AND TURN THE KNOB...

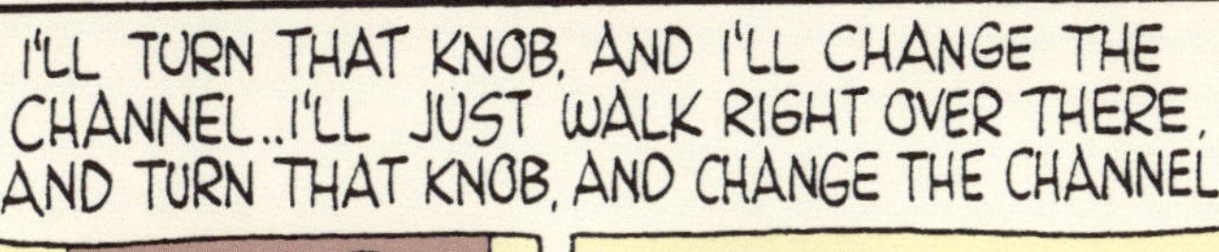
I'LL TURN THAT KNOB, AND I'LL CHANGE THE CHANNEL..I'LL JUST WALK RIGHT OVER THERE, AND TURN THAT KNOB, AND CHANGE THE CHANNEL

THAT'S JUST WHAT I THINK I'LL DO..I THINK I'LL WALK RIGHT OVER THERE, AND TURN THAT KNOB, AND CHANGE THAT CHANNEL...

SCHULZ 3-3
SIGH

MARCH 3, 1957

PEANUTS
by
CHARLES M. SCHULZ
YELL AT IT, CHARLIE BROWN..

WELL, GO AHEAD..

YOU STUPID TREE! LET GO OF THAT KITE!!

YELL AT IT AGAIN..
YOU STUPID TREE! LET GO OF THAT KITE!

NOW GRAB IT, AND SHAKE IT!!

SHAKE IT HARDER..
ARGH!

NOW KICK IT!
WHAM

WHY DO YOU DO EVERYTHING I TELL YOU?
SCHULZ
3-10

PEANUTS
by
CHARLES M. SCHULZ

?
ZOOM!

ZOOM!

♫

AAUGH!

3-17
SCHULZ
YOU DRIVE ME CRAZY!

PEANUTS
by
CHARLES M. SCHULZ
THE YOUNG AND THE OLD..

THE RICH AND THE POOR..

...YESTERDAY, TODAY, TOMORROW AND...

YOU WERE LISTENING TO ME, WEREN'T YOU?
OF COURSE, I WAS!

WELL, I'LL BE!
?

HOW ABOUT THAT?

I'M NOT USED TO HAVING SOMEBODY LISTEN TO WHAT I HAVE TO SAY!
3-24
SCHULZ

PEANUTS
by
CHARLES M. SCHULZ
I THOUGHT I HEARD SOMEBODY IN THE LIVING ROOM?

WHAT'RE YOU DOING UP SO EARLY?

THAT'S MY BALL YOU HAVE THERE..GIVE IT TO ME!
TRY 'N' GET IT!

GIMME IT!

GIMME IT, I SAY!

GIMME IT!

GIMME IT, I SAY!
3-31

WAIT A MINUTE..DO YOU NOTICE ANYTHING PECULIAR?

LOOK UP THERE..

?

NOW, LOOK DOWN THERE...

OH, NO!

WE'RE OUTSIDE!!!
SCHULZ

PEANUTS
by
CHARLES M. SCHULZ

WHOP!

YER **OUT**!
4-7

YOU AND THAT STUPID BLANKET!
SCHULZ

PEANUTS
by
CHARLES M. SCHULZ

GEE, IT WOULD BE NICE TO BE A BIRD!

THEN, IF YOU WEREN'T SATISFIED WHERE YOU WERE, YOU COULD..

..TAKE OFF!

AND THEN IF YOU WEREN'T SATISFIED THERE, YOU COULD **TAKE OFF** AGAIN!

ZOOM!

ZOOM!

ZOOM!

WHEW

I'M NOT SURE I COULD STAND ALL THAT ZOOMING..
4-14
SCHULZ

PEANUTS
by
CHARLES M. SCHULZ

WHAT'S GOING ON HERE?

I'M GIVING LINUS A LITTLE HAND..I'M GOING TO HELP HIM GET HIS KITE IN THE AIR...

YOU?

HA HA HA HA HA HA HA HA HA HA HA HA HA HA...

HO HO HO HO HO HO HO HO HO OH, MY, I CAN'T STAND IT!! HA HA HA HA HA HA HA HA HA HA HA

4-21
SCHULZ

PEANUTS
by
CHARLES M. SCHULZ

HEY! WHERE'S EVERYBODY GOING?

YOU'RE NOT GONNA LET A LITTLE RAIN BOTHER YOU, ARE YA?!
C'MON BACK! IT'S GONNA LET UP! C'MON BACK!!

QUITTERS! THAT'S WHAT YOU ARE!! YOU'RE ALL A BUNCH OF QUITTERS!

?

SIGH
4-28
SCHULZ

PEANUTS
by
CHARLES M. SCHULZ
THE WHOLE TROUBLE WITH YOU IS YOU NEVER LISTEN!
YOU'RE CRAZY!

ALL YOU EVER DO IS TALK!
YOU'RE CRAZY!

I'M RIGHT, AND YOU'RE WRONG! IT'S AS SIMPLE AS THAT!
YOU'RE CRAZY!

OH, YEAH? WELL, LET'S GO HOME RIGHT NOW AND LOOK IN THE DICTIONARY! WE'LL SEE WHO'S CRAZY!

BUT JUST REMEMBER THIS, CHARLIE BROWN... IF I'M RIGHT, I GET 'HITS' ON YOU!!

'HITS'? WHAT IN THE WORLD IS THAT?!
IF I'M RIGHT, I GET TO HIT YOU ON THE ARM!

WELL. WHAT IF I'M RIGHT?! WHAT THEN?!!

THEN YOU GET TO HIT LINUS...
SCHULZ
5-5

PEANUTS
by
CHARLES M. SCHULZ

5-12
SCHULZ

PEANUTS
by
CHARLES M. SCHULZ

WAP!

RUN IT OUT, LINUS! RUN IT OUT!

?
FIRST I GOTTA HAVE MY BLANKET..

STOMP

WHAM

5-19
YOU'RE OUT!!

I CAN'T STAND IT...
SCHULZ

PEANUTS
by
CHARLES M.
SCHULZ

AH...AH....
!

AHHHH...
TURN YOUR HEAD!
TURN YOUR HEAD!
5-26

AHCHOO!

SCHULZ

PEANUTS
by
CHARLES M. SCHULZ

CHARGE!

HEY! WHAT'RE Y'DOING THERE?!!
WHAT'RE Y'DOING WITH THOSE PLIERS?
HEY!

SCHULZ
6-2

PEANUTS
by CHARLES M. SCHULZ
YOU KNOW WHAT?

NO...WHAT?

IT'S DEPRESSING TO REALIZE THAT YOU'RE SO INSIGNIFICANT YOU HAVEN'T GOT A CHANCE EVER TO BECOME PRESIDENT..

IT WOULDN'T BE SO BAD IF I THOUGHT I HAD SOME CHANCE..
WELL, MAYBE YOU HAVE, CHARLIE BROWN...

MAYBE THROUGH SOME FANTASTIC STROKE OF LUCK, YOU'LL GET TO BE PRESIDENT!

MAYBE THROUGH SOME BIZARRE TWIST OF FATE, YOU'LL BE ELECTED!

MAYBE THROUGH THE MOST OUTRAGEOUS, MONSTROUS AND ATROCIOUS TURN OF HISTORICAL EVENTS, YOU'LL BE PLACED IN THE WHITE HOUSE!!!

MAYBE THROUGH THE MOST HIDEOUS..
GOOD GRIEF!!
SCHULZ
6-9

PEANUTS
by SCHULZ

GULP

SNOOPY'S THE ONLY DOG IN THE WORLD WHO CAN RETRIEVE A SOAP-BUBBLE..

GULP

6-16

OF COURSE, IT'S NOT ONE OF THOSE THINGS YOU CAN DO ALL DAY LONG!
SCHULZ

PEANUTS
by
CHARLES M. SCHULZ

SAY! I THOUGHT WE WERE GONNA TAKE TURNS USING THAT UMBRELLA?

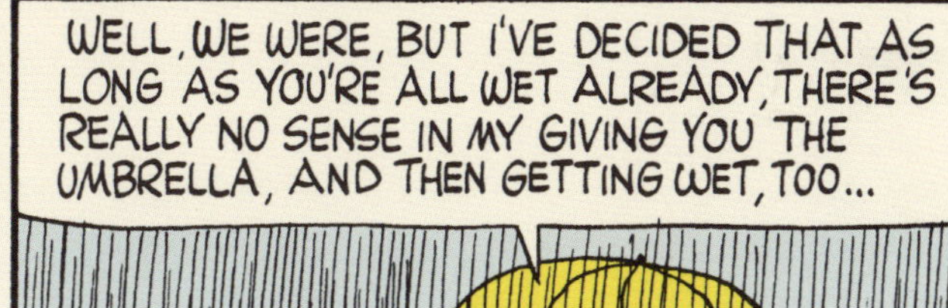
WELL, WE WERE, BUT I'VE DECIDED THAT AS LONG AS YOU'RE ALL WET ALREADY, THERE'S REALLY NO SENSE IN MY GIVING YOU THE UMBRELLA, AND THEN GETTING WET, TOO...

THAT WOULDN'T MAKE SENSE, WOULD IT? NO, IT WOULDN'T...

SO MUCH IN THIS WORLD DEPENDS UPON WHO GETS BORN FIRST!
6-23
SCHULZ

PEANUTS
by
CHARLES M. SCHULZ

Z

?

6-30
SCHULZ

PEANUTS
by
CHARLES M. SCHULZ

GET AWAY FROM THOSE CRAYONS!!

MOM!

OH, GOOD GRIEF!!
LUCY! YOU SHARE THOSE CRAYONS WITH YOUR BROTHER!

BOY, I OUGHTA SLUG YOU A GOOD ONE!
JUST GIVE ME THE CRAYONS..

HERE'S THREE OF 'EM... NOW, GET OUTA HERE!

♪

I GAVE HIM THREE, MOM.. WAS THAT ENOUGH?
THAT WAS FINE, LUCY.. IT'S ALWAYS NICE TO SHARE YOUR THINGS...
SCHULZ

WHITE, GRAY AND BLACK *SIGH*
7-7

PEANUTS
by CHARLES M. SCHULZ
DO YOU KNOW ANYTHING ABOUT MULES?

I'VE BEEN READING ABOUT THEM..

Z

THEY SAY THAT THE MULE IS A VERY **POWERFUL** ANIMAL..
Z

THAT'S TRUE... I'VE HEARD THAT THEY CAN ACTUALLY KICK DOWN BARN DOORS!

KICK DOWN BARN DOORS?
UH, HUH..

THAT'S FANTASTIC!
I KNOW IT IS, BUT IT'S TRUE!

RIDICULOUS!
7-14
SCHULZ

PEANUTS
by
CHARLES M. SCHULZ

WHOOPS!

WHAM!

WHEW!

SCHULZ
7-21
SEE WHAT YOU MADE ME DO?!

I CAN'T STAND IT! I JUST CAN'T STAND IT!
PEANUTS
by CHARLES M. SCHULZ

YOU STUPID TREE! LET GO OF THAT KITE!

LET GO, I SAY, OR I'LL GIVE YOU THE WORST SHAKING YOU'VE EVER HAD!

7-28

IS IT AUTUMN?
SCHULZ

PEANUTS
by
CHARLES M. SCHULZ

BEETHOVEN! PHOOEY! HE WASN'T SO GREAT!

WHAT DO YOU MEAN, HE WASN'T SO GREAT?!

WELL, HE DIDN'T GET TO BE KING, DID HE? HUH?

HE DIDN'T GET TO BE KING, DID HE? HUH? DID HE???
8-4

DID HE GET TO BE KING? HUH? DID HE? DID HE?!!
SCHULZ

GOOD GRIEF!
HOW CAN ANYONE BE CALLED 'GREAT' IF HE DOESN'T GET TO BE KING?

PEANUTS
by
CHARLES M. SCHULZ

OWOO

OOOOO

SLAM!

?

Z
SCHULZ
8-11

PEANUTS
by
CHARLES M. SCHULZ

THE REASON I CAN GUARANTEE THIS PARACHUTE, CHARLIE BROWN, IS THAT I MADE IT MYSELF..

THIS IS A GOOD HEAVY BLANKET, AND THESE ARE VERY STOUT ROPES..
PUT MY CAP ON FOR ME, WILL YOU?

THERE..NOW, ALL YOU HAVE TO DO IS JUMP OFF THAT STUMP, AND FLOAT GENTLY TO THE GROUND..

JUST WHAT I WAS AFRAID OF.. HE'S GETTING COLD FEET...

GERONIMO!
WUMP!
8-18

MMGBMM MGMMBM MMGMM

I THINK I'D BETTER GO HOME, AN' SEE WHAT'S ON T.V.
SCHULZ

PEANUTS
by CHARLES M. SCHULZ

LUCY, HAVE YOU SEEN LINUS?

HE'S DOWN THERE BY THE WATER, THROWING STONES...

EVERY TIME WE COME TO THE BEACH, HE SPENDS THE WHOLE DAY THROWING STONES INTO THE WATER..

HAVING FUN, LINUS?
SORT OF...

WHAT DO YOU MEAN, 'SORT OF'?

SCHULZ
8-25
I HAVE A HARD TIME GETTING ANY DISTANCE..

PEANUTS
by
CHARLES M.
SCHULZ
SIX O'CLOCK AGAIN..

GOOD GRIEF!

I HATE IT WHEN IT'S TIME TO FEED SNOOPY!

I HATE IT!

I HATE IT! I HATE IT!
I HATE IT!

SNOOPY! SUPPERTIME!!

BREAD
ZOOM!
ZOOM!
GULP!

I JUST **HATE** IT!!
9-1
SCHULZ

PEANUTS
by
CHARLES M. SCHULZ

TICKLE TICKLE

HE HE HE
TICKLE TICKLE TICKLE

HE HE HE
TICKLE TICKLE TICKLE

HE HE HE HE HE HE HE HE HE
TICKLE TICKLE TICKLE TICKLE

HE HE HE HE HE HE HE HE HE HE HE HE HE

HE HE HE HE HE HE HE HE HE..

HE HE HE HE HE HE HE HE HE HE

HE HE HE HE HE HE HE HE HE HE HE HE HE
?
SNOOPY
9-8
SCHULZ

PEANUTS
by
CHARLES M. SCHULZ

CLOMP
ZOOM!

ZOOM!

WHOOSH!
ZOOM!

WOOSH!
WHOOSH!
WHOOSH!

SCHULZ
9-15

PEANUTS
by CHARLES M. SCHULZ
NO!

ABSOLUTELY NOT!

YOU MUST THINK I'M CRAZY!

YOU SAY YOU'LL HOLD THE BALL, BUT YOU **WON'T**! YOU'LL PULL IT AWAY, AND I'LL BREAK MY NECK!
WHY, CHARLIE BROWN.. HOW YOU TALK...

I WOULDN'T **THINK** OF SUCH A THING! I'M A **CHANGED** PERSON! LOOK...ISN'T THIS A FACE YOU CAN TRUST?

ALL RIGHT...YOU HOLD THE BALL, AND I'LL COME RUNNING UP, AND KICK IT...

SHE DID IT AGAIN!!

WUMP!

SCHULZ
9-22
I ADMIRE YOU, CHARLIE BROWN... YOU HAVE SUCH FAITH IN HUMAN NATURE..

PEANUTS
by
CHARLES M. SCHULZ

ZZ

AHEM

THAT'S MY BLANKET YOU'RE SLEEPING ON, YOU STUPID DOG!

YAWN!

Z

HEY! WHO LET ALL THOSE CATS IN HERE?

9-29
SCHULZ

PEANUTS
by
CHARLES M. SCHULZ

THERE!

I HAVE A SURPRISE FOR YOU, SCHROEDER..

WHAT IS IT?
A PICTURE OF BEETHOVEN! I DREW IT MYSELF!

WELL, I'LL BE!! THIS IS SWELL!
I THOUGHT MAYBE YOU'D LIKE TO HAVE IT-TO HANG IN YOUR ROOM..

THAT'S A GOOD IDEA..
I'M SO HAPPY THAT YOU LIKE IT, SCHROEDER.. I WOULD HAVE BEEN SO DISAPPOINTED IF YOU HADN'T...

NOW, WHERE DO YOU THINK I SHOULD HANG IT?
!
10-6

HANG IT AROUND YOUR NECK, YOU BLOCKHEAD!
SCHULZ

PEANUTS
by
CHARLES M. SCHULZ
SIGH
GEE... I WISH I COULD GO TO SCHOOL..
I FEEL A NEED TO BE EDUCATED..
I WANT TO LEARN TO READ AND TO WRITE AND TO KNOW ALL ABOUT HISTORY..
10-13
I HAVE A **RIGHT** TO BE EDUCATED!
SCHULZ
IN FACT, I **DEMAND** TO BE EDUCATED!!
KLUNK!

PEANUTS
by CHARLES M. SCHULZ

WUMP!
OOF!

BEST SAFETY-MAN WE'VE EVER HAD!
10-20
SCHULZ

NOW'S THE TIME FOR A GOOD PASS PLAY!
PEANUTS
by CHARLES M. SCHULZ
ALL RIGHT, MEN, LET'S GET IN THERE THIS TIME, AND SMEAR 'EM!

NOW, LISTEN CAREFULLY

SCHROEDER HIKES THE BALL TO YOU, LINUS, AND YOU FADE BACK, AND THROW ME A LONG PASS..

NOW, ARE YOU SURE YOU UNDERSTAND?

OF COURSE, I UNDERSTAND!
WELL, I HOPE SO..

SIGNALS! THIRTY-THREE! EIGHTEEN! FORTY-NINE!

HIKE!

PASS IT!

10-27

SCHULZ

PEANUTS
by CHARLES M. SCHULZ
THUMP!

CLUMP!

YOU WOULDN'T HIT A GIRL, WOULD YOU?
HUH?

WHOP!

GOOD GRIEF!

HERE, CHARLIE BROWN... I'M RETURNING YOUR HITTING GLOVES...

THESE AREN'T "HITTING" GLOVES...THESE ARE "BOXING" GLOVES

THERE WASN'T ANY BOXING.. THERE WAS ONLY HITTING!
SCHULZ

PEANUTS
CHARLES M. SCHULZ
IS THAT YOUR HEAD, CHARLIE BROWN, OR IS THE MOON OUT EARLY TODAY?

BOY, YOU SURE THINK YOU'RE SMART, DON'T YOU?

I OUGHTA SOCK YOU RIGHT ON THE NOSE!
11-10

YOU CAN'T HIT ME, CHARLIE BROWN! I'M A GIRL!

NYAHH!!!

NYAH NYAH NYAH NYAH!

?

HERE, NOW! YOU STOP THAT! STOP THAT, I SAY!!

YOU STOP KICKING OUR HOUSE!
SCHULZ

PEANUTS
by CHARLES M. SCHULZ
YOU AND YOUR INSULTS!

BOY, IF YOU WEREN'T A GIRL...

I OUGHTA SLUG YOU A GOOD ONE!

ALL RIGHT, CHARLIE BROWN! COME ON, AND TRY IT!

YOU'RE ALWAYS TALKING BIG! NOW, C'MON! TRY IT!!

FIGHT! FIGHT!
OH, GOOD GRIEF!
C'MON, CHARLIE BROWN! PUT 'EM UP!
FIGHT!

C'MON.. I'M READY FOR YOU! PUT 'EM UP THERE!!

A PERSON SHOULDN'T HAVE TO LOSE ALL HIS PRIDE WHEN HE'S ONLY SIX YEARS OLD...
11-17
SCHULZ

PEANUTS
By
CHARLES M. SCHULZ

CLOMP!

SNOOPY

11-24
SCHULZ

PEANUTS
by SCHULZ

AHEM!

12-1
SIGH
SCHULZ

PEANUTS
by CHARLES M. SCHULZ
BOY, YOU SURE TALK A LOT!
YEAH? WELL, I'M NOT ALL TALK LIKE SOME PEOPLE I KNOW!

GOOD GRIEF! HOW DO I GET INTO THESE THINGS?
DO YOU WANNA PUT 'EM UP?

C'MON, CHARLIE BROWN, LET'S SEE WHAT YOU'RE MADE OF!

C'MON, PUT 'EM UP, HERE! WHAT'S THE MATTER WITH YOU? PUT 'EM UP!

YOU SHOULD'A' SLUGGED HER, CHARLIE BROWN! EVEN IF SHE IS MY SISTER, I SAY YOU SHOULD HAVE SLUGGED HER!

YOU DON'T UNDERSTAND, LINUS... CHARLIE BROWN DID A VERY ADMIRABLE THING.. HE WOULD NEVER THINK OF HITTING A GIRL, SO HE DELIBERATELY HUMILIATED HIMSELF TO HOLD ON TO HIS HIGH MORAL STANDARDS!
12-8

ISN'T THAT RIGHT, CHARLIE BROWN?
NO, I WAS JUST AFRAID OF GETTING BEAT UP!
SCHULZ

HE SHOULD BE RIGHT ALONG HERE..
PEANUTS
by CHARLES M. SCHULZ

WHO SHOULD BE RIGHT ALONG WHERE?

AH! HERE HE IS!! MY PAL!

HOW SICKENING!
MY BUDDY! MY GOOD BUDDY! MY OL' BUDDY!!

MY TRUE FRIEND!
HOW REVOLTING!

EVERY DAY WHEN I COME HOME FROM SCHOOL, HE ACTS THIS WAY...HE'S SO GLAD TO SEE ME!
WHY DON'T YOU TELL HIM TODAY IS SUNDAY, AND YOU HAVEN'T BEEN TO SCHOOL?

12-15
SCHULZ

PEANUTS
by CHARLES M. SCHULZ
DISGRACEFUL!

I JUST CAN'T STAND IT!!

?
ZIP!

RIP!

RIP! RIP! RIP!

THAT'S WHAT I THINK OF YOU AND YOUR STUPID BLANKET!

SIGH

SCHULZ
12-22

PEANUTS
by
CHARLES M. SCHULZ

12-29

WHAM!

SCHULZ
ONE PATCH OF ICE DOTH NOT A WINTER MAKE..
OH, SHUT UP!

PEANUTS
by
CHARLES M. SCHULZ

!

IT'S HAPPENING, CHARLIE BROWN! IT'S HAPPENING JUST LIKE THEY SAID IT WOULD!!

OF COURSE, IT'S HAPPENING.. IT'S SNOWING..WHAT ELSE DID YOU EXPECT THIS TIME OF YEAR?

SNOWING?

GOOD GRIEF..I THOUGHT IT WAS THE FALLOUT!
1-5
SCHULZ

PEANUTS®
by
CHARLES M. SCHULZ

BOY, HOW THAT GIRL CAN DANCE! SHE'S REALLY A BALL OF FIRE! YES, SIR! SHE'S QUITE A GIRL!!

TOO BAD SHE ISN'T A DOG..
SNOOPY
1-12
SCHULZ

YOU KNOW WHAT?
PEANUTS
by CHARLES M. SCHULZ
WHAT?

NINETY-TWO, NINETY-THREE, NINETY-FOUR..

IT SAYS HERE THAT THE YOUTH OF TODAY IS BADLY OUT OF CONDITION..
..NINETY-FIVE!

...NINETY-SIX, NINETY-SEVEN, NINETY-EIGHT, NINETY-NINE..

ONE HUNDRED!

ONE HUNDRED AN' ONE, ONE HUNDRED AN' TWO, ONE HUNDRED AN' THREE, ONE HUNDRED AN' FOUR, ONE HUNDRED AN' FIVE..

FIRST WITH THE LEFT, AND THEN WITH THE RIGHT... ONE HUNDRED AN' SIX, ONE HUNDRED AN' SEVEN, ONE HUNDRED AN' EIGHT..

I DON'T KNOW ABOUT YOUTH, BUT WE LITTLE KIDS ARE IN GREAT SHAPE!
1-19
SCHULZ

PEANUTS
by
CHARLES M. SCHULZ
WHAT ARE YOU MAKING?
THESE ARE SNOW-BUNNIES

THEY LOOK REAL CUTE..

CAN I HELP YOU, LUCY?

NO, YOU CAN'T HELP ME! GET OUT OF HERE! MAKE YOUR OWN THINGS!!

AND DON'T BOTHER ME ANY MORE! DO YOU HEAR ME?

LITTLE BROTHERS CAN SURE BE A NUISANCE SOMETIMES!

SCHULZ
1-26

PEANUTS
by
CHARLES M. SCHULZ

THERE'S SOMETHING ABOUT SEEING THAT STUPID KID WITH THAT BLANKET THAT GALLS ME!

CLOMP!

2-2

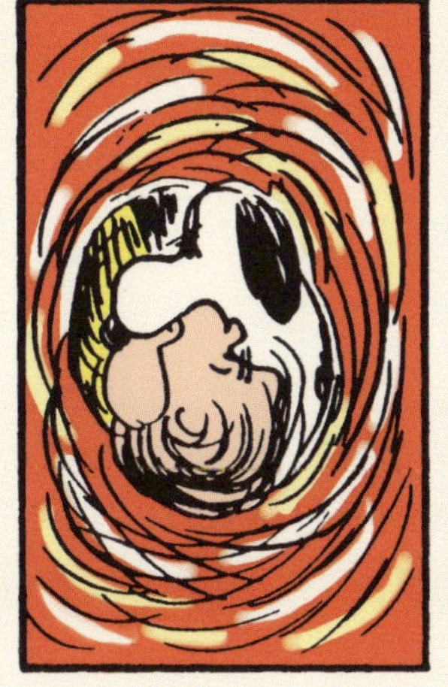

WHAM!

SCHULZ
SECURITY, LIKE LIBERTY, HAS TO BE WON AND REWON MANY TIMES...
BEAT AGAIN!

PEANUTS
by
CHARLES M. SCHULZ

2-9

SIGH
SCHULZ

PEANUTS
by
CHARLES M. SCHULZ

2-16

SCHULZ
BUT IS IT ART?

PEANUTS
by CHARLES M. SCHULZ
HI, CHARLIE BROWN... HOW'S THE FRIEND OF ALL MANKIND?
HA HA HA

GOOD GRIEF!
HA HA HA HA!

WELL, IF IT ISN'T CHARLIE BROWN!

GOOD OL' WISHY-WASHY CHARLIE BROWN!

HA HA HA HA HA!

HI, CHARLIE BROWN... IS THAT YOUR HEAD, OR ARE YOU HIDING BEHIND A BALLOON?

HAHAHAHAHAHA

CLICK!

"...AND WHAT, IN ALL THIS WORLD, IS MORE DELIGHTFUL THAN THE GAY WONDERFUL LAUGHTER OF LITTLE CHILDREN?"

2-23
SCHULZ

!
PEANUTS
by
CHARLES M. SCHULZ
YAWN!

CLOMP!

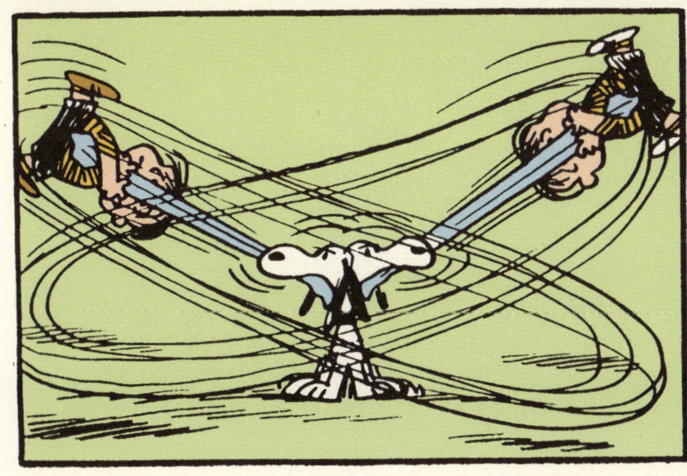

AND THERE HE GOES!
WHOOSH!

3-2

I'M THE FIRST DOG EVER TO LAUNCH A HUMAN BEING!
SCHULZ

MARCH 2, 1958

!
PEANUTS
by
CHARLES M. SCHULZ
ZIP
GOAL!

WHAT'S THE MATTER WITH YOU ANYWAY?!
YOU LET IT GO RIGHT THROUGH YOU!!

GO ON HOME, CHARLIE BROWN! WE DON'T WANT YOU ON OUR SIDE!

RATS!

I CAN'T DO ANYTHING RIGHT!

I CAN'T PLAY HOCKEY, I CAN'T PLAY CHECKERS, I CAN'T FLY KITES, I CAN'T DO ANYTHING RIGHT!

WHAT'S THE MATTER, CHARLIE BROWN?
OH, I DON'T KNOW...I'M DEPRESSED...I DON'T FEEL GOOD...I THINK MAYBE I'M GETTING THE ASIAN FLU..

THE ASIAN FLU? THAT'S BEEN OVER FOR SIX MONTHS!

HA HA HA HA!! WHAT A GUY! EVERYONE ELSE GOT THE ASIAN FLU SIX MONTHS AGO, AND HE'S JUST GETTING IT NOW! HA HA HA!

GOOD GRIEF! I CAN'T EVEN GET SICK RIGHT!
3-9
SCHULZ

PEANUTS
by
CHARLES M. SCHULZ
STOP LICKING MY HANDS!

GET OUT OF HERE!

Hey!

GET AWAY FROM ME WITH YOUR OL' WET TONGUE!

HEY! CUT IT OUT!!

DO YOU HAVE TO BE LICKING PEOPLE ALL THE TIME?!

IF YOU'RE NOT LICKING SOMEBODY'S HANDS, YOU'RE LICKING SOMEBODY'S SHOES!

STUPID DOG!
3-16

THEY ALL RESENT ME BECAUSE I'M SO DEVOTED!
SCHULZ

PEANUTS
by
CHARLES M. SCHULZ
WHAT ARE YOU WATCHING?
NONE OF YOUR BUSINESS!

I WANNA WATCH **MY** PROGRAM..

GET OUT OF HERE!

YOU ALWAYS GET TO WATCH YOUR PROGRAMS, AND I NEVER GET TO WATCH MY PROGRAMS..

DO YOU WANNA GET HIT?! I'LL SLUG YOU A GOOD ONE!

BROTHER OR NO BROTHER, I'LL RUN ROUGHSHOD OVER YOU!!
3-23

WHAT ARE YOU DOING?
I'M TURNING OFF YOUR PROGRAM, AND TURNING ON MINE..

YOU DON'T FRIGHTEN ME ONE BIT!

SCHULZ
WAAH!

OH, OH!
PEANUTS
by CHARLES M. SCHULZ

HERE IT COMES!

HEY! WHERE'S EVERYBODY GOING?
HOME! IT'S RAINING YOU BLOCKHEAD!

COME BACK HERE!
THIS IS ONLY A SPRING SHOWER!

QUITTERS!
ARE YOU AFRAID OF A LITTLE WATER?

QUITTERS!
QUITTERS!
QUITTERS!
QUITTERS!

WELL, AT LEAST LINUS, MY FAITHFUL RIGHT-FIELDER, HASN'T DESERTED ME....HE'S STILL..

3-30
SCHULZ

PEANUTS
by CHARLES M. SCHULZ

WHAT'S THAT, SCHROEDER?
THIS IS A NEW RECORDING OF BRAHMS' FOURTH SYMPHONY..

WHAT ARE YOU GOING TO DO WITH IT?
I'M GOING TO TAKE IT HOME, AND LISTEN TO IT..

YOU MEAN YOU'RE GOING TO DANCE TO IT?
NO, I'M JUST GOING TO LISTEN TO IT..
BRAHMS

ARE YOU GOING TO MARCH AROUND THE ROOM WHILE YOU LISTEN TO IT?
NO, I'M JUST GOING TO SIT, AND LISTEN TO IT..
BRAHMS

YOU MEAN YOU'RE GOING TO WHISTLE OR SING WHILE YOU LISTEN TO IT?
NO, I'M JUST GOING TO LISTEN TO IT..
BRAHMS

THAT'S THE MOST RIDICULOUS THING I'VE EVER HEARD!
4-6
SCHULZ

PEANUTS
by
CHARLES M. SCHULZ
Z

Z

Z

4-13
SCHULZ
GOOD GRIEF!
Z

PEANUTS
by
CHARLES M. SCHULZ
YOU NEVER GIVE UP, DO YOU, CHARLIE BROWN?
NOPE!

WHY SHOULD I?

I'M GOING TO GET THIS KITE UP IN THE AIR IF IT KILLS ME!

AAGH

OOOOO!

AAGGHH!

ARGHRRG

GASP!
SIGH

DON'T SAY ANYTHING.. JUST GO GET A SCISSORS!
4-20
SCHULZ

APRIL 27, 1958

PEANUTS
by
CHARLES M. SCHULZ

DID YOU GET THAT KITE UP ALL BY YOURSELF, LINUS?
YUP!

DID YOU HAVE ANY TROUBLE?
NOPE!

DIDN'T YOUR KITE GET TANGLED UP IN ANY TREES OR AROUND SOME TELEPHONE WIRES OR EVEN GO DOWN A SEWER?
NOPE!

SIGH

I DIDN'T THINK IT WOULD BE RIGHT TO LET A LITTLE KID LIKE HIM SEE ME CRY..
SCHULZ
5-4

PEANUTS
by
CHARLES M. SCHULZ

Whop!

5-11
SCHULZ

YOU NITWIT! YOU BIRDBRAIN!
PEANUTS
by CHARLES M. SCHULZ

WHY DON'T YOU GO JUMP IN THE LAKE?

YOU'RE NOT SO SMART!

YOU BLOCKHEAD! YOU NUMSKULL!

YOU THINK YOU'RE SO SMART! WELL, YOU'RE NOT! YOU'RE STUPID!! DO YOU HEAR ME? YOU'RE STUPID!

CHARLIE BROWN, CAN YOU SEE WHO THAT IS?

NO...THEY'RE TOO FAR AWAY... I CAN'T MAKE OUT WHO IT IS..

I FORGOT WHO I WAS YELLING AT!
5-18
SCHULZ

PEANUTS
by
CHARLES M. SCHULZ

CLOMP!
AAUGH!

5-25

NO MANAGER IN THE HISTORY OF BASEBALL HAS EVER HAD TO GO THROUGH WHAT I HAVE TO GO THROUGH!
SCHULZ

PEANUTS
by CHARLES M. SCHULZ
WELL!

LOOK, SCHROEDER..THEY PRINTED MY LETTER IN THE PAPER..

"DEAR AGNES, I AM IN LOVE WITH A BOY WHO DOESN'T EVEN KNOW I AM ALIVE."

"ALL HE EVER SEEMS TO THINK OF IS HIS STUPID PIANO AND THAT STUPID OL' BEETHOVEN!"

"CAN YOU GIVE ME ANY ADVICE?"

KLUNK!

AND HERE'S HER ANSWER..."DEAR, LUCY,....NEVER FALL IN LOVE WITH A MUSICIAN." HMMM... I KIND OF SUSPECTED THAT...
SCHULZ
6-1

PEANUTS
by
CHARLES M. SCHULZ
OH, NO!!!

THIS IS THE LAST STRAW!

DID YOU DRAW THIS PICTURE IN MY BOOK?

I GUESS I DID.....

IT'S A PRETTY NICE PICTURE, DON'T YOU THINK? SEE, THERE'S A KNIGHT ON HORSEBACK AND THERE'S A BIG DRAGON, AND...

WHO DO YOU THINK YOU ARE?

WHAT CAN I SAY?
Furry Tails

THIS IS MY BOOK, AND YOU HAVE DRAWN A PICTURE IN IT... NOW, I WANT TO KNOW WHAT YOU'RE GOING TO DO ABOUT IT!
Furry Tails
6-8

Furry Tails

DO YOU WANT ME TO SIGN IT?
Furry Tails

I THINK I SAID THE WRONG THING!
BONK!
Furry Tails
SCHULZ

PEANUTS
by SCHULZ

HERE COMES THE FIERCE TIGER SNEAKING UP ON THE HELPLESS CHILD...

SUDDENLY HE POUNCES!

SUDDENLY HE POUNCES!

6-15
RATS!
SCHULZ

PEANUTS
by
CHARLES M. SCHULZ
Z

6-22
SCHULZ

PEANUTS
by
CHARLES M. SCHULZ

WHAM!

6-29
SCHULZ

PEANUTS
by
CHARLES M. SCHULZ
MY DAD IS TALLER THAN YOUR DAD..

MY DAD HAS BROADER SHOULDERS THAN YOUR DAD..

MY DAD IS BETTER LOOKING THAN YOUR DAD

YOUR DAD!! YOU'RE ALWAYS TALKING ABOUT YOUR DAD!!

MAYBE MY DAD ISN'T PERFECT, BUT I LIKE HIM ANYWAY!!

HE'S MY DAD, AND I LIKE HIM!!!

YOU'RE SCREAMING, CHARLIE BROWN..
I'M SORRY... I DIDN'T MEAN TO SCREAM..

I WAS ONLY TRYING TO SAY THAT I LIKE MY DAD FOR WHAT HE IS... HE'S MY DAD, AND I LIKE HIM...

THAT'S VERY COMMENDABLE, CHARLIE BROWN... YOU ARE TO BE CONGRATULATED ON YOUR LOYALTY..
THANK YOU
7-6

HOWEVER, MY DAD...
OH, GOOD GRIEF!
SCHULZ

PEANUTS
by
CHARLES M. SCHULZ

7-13

SCHULZ

PHOOEY!
PEANUTS
by
CHARLES M. SCHULZ

I FEEL MEAN TODAY!

WHEN I FEEL MEAN, NOBODY BETTER GET IN MY WAY!

7-20
NOBODY!
SCHULZ

THIS IS A PRESENT FOR VIOLET, BUT I'M SURE NOT GOING TO TELL **YOU** WHAT IT IS!

PEANUTS
THIS IS HOPELESS!

A BLOODHOUND COULDN'T FIND ANYTHING OUT HERE!

I CAN'T FIND THE BALL!

WADDYA MEAN, PICK IT UP?!

HOW DO YOU EXPECT ANYONE TO FIND A BALL IN WEEDS LIKE THESE? WHAT DID YOU HIT IT OUT HERE FOR?

IT'S IMPOSSIBLE! OF COURSE, I'M LOOKING! I SAID I CAN'T FIND IT! IF I COULD FIND IT, WOULD I STILL BE OUT HERE?

THIS IS HOPELESS! NOBODY COULD FIND ANYTHING OUT HERE! YOU COULDN'T FIND A BATTLESHIP OUT HERE IF IT..

..WAIT A MINUTE...

I FOUND IT...
SCHULZ

PEANUTS®
by
CHARLES M. SCHULZ

YOU'RE SLOWING DOWN, "PIG-PEN"...

WAIT A MINUTE...I THINK THERE'S SOME SAND IN MY SHOES...

THERE...THAT'S BETTER!

8-10
I JUST CAN'T RUN IF I HAVE SOMETHING IN MY SHOE...
good grief!
SCHULZ

CONE
SUNDAE
ICE
CREAM
PEANUTS
by
CHARLES M. SCHULZ

8-17
YOU DRIVE
ME CRAZY!
SCHULZ

PEANUTS
by
CHARLES M. SCHULZ

CLOMP!

SNOOPY

SNOOPY

8-24

SCHULZ

AUGUST 31, 1958

PEANUTS
by
SCHULZ
SIGH THERE'S NOBODY AS FASCINATING AS A MUSICIAN...

WELL...IT'S NOW OR NEVER...

AHEM

YOU KNOW, SCHROEDER...HEE HEE HEE HEE....IF YOU EVER WANTED TO...HEE HEE HEE... LEAN OVER, AND KISS ME... HEE HEE HEE HEE... I WOULDN'T MIND...

GOOD GRIEF!
I MEAN... HEE HEE HEE... IF YOU REALLY WANTED TO... ..HEE HEE HEE HEE HEE...

I MEAN....AFTER ALL... THERE'S NOTHING WRONG WITH A LITTLE KISS BETWEEN FRIENDS...

ON THE EAR...WHY, HOW QUAINT...HOW LIKE A MUSICIAN...
SMACK!

GERMS! DISEASE!! INFECTION!!!

I'VE NEVER BEEN SO INSULTED IN ALL MY LIFE!
9-7
SCHULZ

PEANUTS
by
CHARLES M. SCHULZ

!
!

9-14

MY MOTHER DIDN'T RAISE ME TO SPEND MY WHOLE LIFE CHASING STICKS!
SCHULZ

PEANUTS
by
CHARLES M. SCHULZ

YOU SHOULD TRY SOME 'PLACE-KICKS'...

WHY DON'T YOU LET ME HOLD THE BALL FOR YOU, CHARLIE BROWN?

DO YOU THINK I'M CRAZY? DO YOU THINK YOU CAN FOOL ME WITH THE SAME TRICK EVERY YEAR?!

OH, I WON'T PULL THE BALL AWAY, CHARLIE BROWN.. I PROMISE YOU... I GIVE YOU MY BONDED WORD!

ALL RIGHT, I'LL TRUST YOU... I HAVE AN UNDYING FAITH IN HUMAN NATURE!

I BELIEVE THAT PEOPLE WHO WANT TO CHANGE CAN DO SO, AND I BELIEVE THAT THEY SHOULD BE GIVEN A CHANCE TO PROVE THEMSELVES..
9-21

AAUGH!

WUMP!

CHARLIE BROWN, YOUR FAITH IN HUMAN NATURE IS AN INSPIRATION TO ALL YOUNG PEOPLE..
SCHULZ

PEANUTS
by
CHARLES M. SCHULZ

LUCY, WILL YOU READ THIS BOOK TO ME?
NO!

AW, C'MON..
NO!

PLEEEEEEZ?

"A MAN WAS BORN...HE LIVED AND HE DIED!"

9-28
"THE END!"

WHAT A FASCINATING ACCOUNT...

IT ALMOST MAKES YOU WISH YOU HAD KNOWN THE FELLOW..
SCHULZ

PEANUTS
by SCHULZ
Z

TICKLE TICKLE TICKLE

TICKLE TICKLE TICKLE TICKLE
HEE HEE HEE HEE HEE

OH, NOT ON THE FEET! OH, NO! PLEASE! NOT ON THE FEET!!
HEE HEE HEE
TICKLE! TICKLE! TICKLE!

HEE HEE HEE HEE HEE HEE

OH, MAN! I'M EXHAUSTED! OH, MY RIBS! OH, MAN! WHEW

I HAVEN'T LAUGHED SO MUCH IN A YEAR...WHAT A GIRL! WOW!
10-5

IT MUST BE NICE TO BE ABLE TO BRING SO MUCH HAPPINESS INTO SOMEONE'S LIFE..
SCHULZ

PEANUTS
by SCHULZ

MAY I HELP YOU WITH YOUR PUZZLE, LUCY?

NO! BESIDES, I'M ALMOST DONE..
PLEASE?

OH, GOOD GRIEF! ALL RIGHT! HERE...YOU CAN PUT IN THE LAST PIECE..

GOOD! NOW, LET ME SEE.. HOW DOES IT GO? DOES IT FIT LIKE THIS, OR DOES IT FIT LIKE THIS? OR MAYBE DOES IT FIT THIS WAY? LET'S SEE NOW...
?

DOES IT FIT THIS WAY OR THIS WAY OR THIS WAY? OR MAYBE DOES IT FIT THAT WAY?
10-12

MAYBE IT FITS LIKE THIS OR AROUND THIS WAY OR MAYBE IT FITS THIS WAY OR LIKE THIS OR MAYBE..

GIMME THAT PIECE!!

SHE NEVER LETS ME HELP WITH ANYTHING..
SCHULZ

AND DON'T COME BACK!
PEANUTS
by SCHULZ

GET OUT OF HERE!

MAN, WHAT A DAY! PEOPLE HAVE BEEN YELLING AT ME EVER SINCE I GOT UP THIS MORNING!

WHEN YOU'RE DISTRAUGHT, THERE'S NOTHING THAT WILL RELAX YOU LIKE LYING WITH YOUR HEAD IN YOUR WATER DISH...

THIS IS REALLY NOT A NEW TEACHING, FOR IT WAS PRACTICED AS LONG AGO AS THE TWELFTH CENTURY..

?
SNIFF SNIFF... WHAT IN THE WORLD?

!

ORANGE JUICE!
10-19
SCHULZ

PEANUTS
IF YOU THINK YOU'RE GETTING AWAY WITH SOMETHING, YOU'RE MISTAKEN!

YOU'RE NOT INSCRUTABLE, YOU KNOW!

YOU CAN'T PUT ANYTHING OVER ON ME!

I KNOW JUST WHAT YOU'RE THINKING!

I CAN SEE RIGHT THROUGH YOU! YOU'RE TRANSPARENT!!

SIGH

10-26
I HAVE A GLASS HEAD!
SCHULZ

PEANUTS
by SCHULZ
WOW... I'VE NEVER EATEN SO MUCH CHICKEN BEFORE IN ALL MY LIFE!

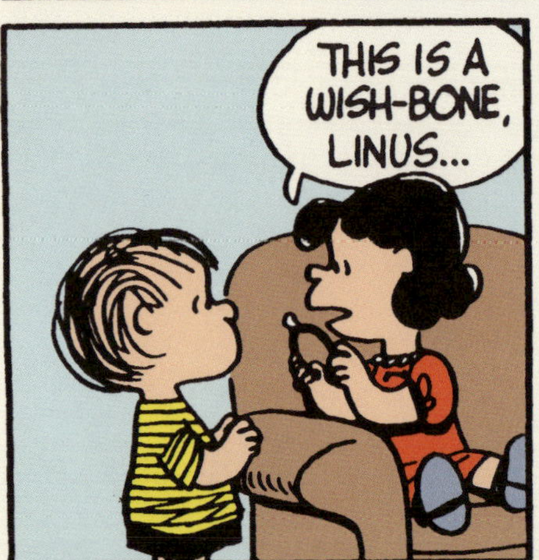
THIS IS A WISH-BONE, LINUS...

WE BOTH MAKE OUR WISHES, AND THEN WE PULL IT APART... WHOEVER BREAKS OFF THE BIGGEST PART GETS HIS WISH..

DO WE WISH OUT LOUD?
OF COURSE, WE WISH OUT LOUD!

IF YOU DON'T WISH OUT LOUD, THE "WISH-ANSWERER" WON'T KNOW WHAT TO BRING YOU!

I APOLOGIZE FOR BEING SO STUPID..

LET'S SEE NOW... I WISH FOR A NEW DOLL, A NEW BICYCLE, FOUR NEW SWEATERS, SOME NEW SADDLE SHOES, A WRIST WATCH AND ABOUT A HUNDRED DOLLARS!

I WISH FOR A LONG LIFE FOR ALL MY FRIENDS, I WISH FOR PEACE IN THE WORLD, I WISH FOR GREATER ADVANCEMENTS IN THE FIELDS OF SCIENCE AND MEDICINE AND I...

YOU SEEM TO HAVE A KNACK FOR SPOILING EVERYTHING!
11-2
SCHULZ

PEANUTS
by
CHARLES M. SCHULZ
READY?

READY!

..TAKE A DEEP BREATH... NOW HOLD IT!

WOOOSH!

WOOSH!!

11-9
SCHULZ

THERE IT IS! YES, SIR... WOW!
PEANUTS
by CHARLES M. SCHULZ

HOW ABOUT THAT?

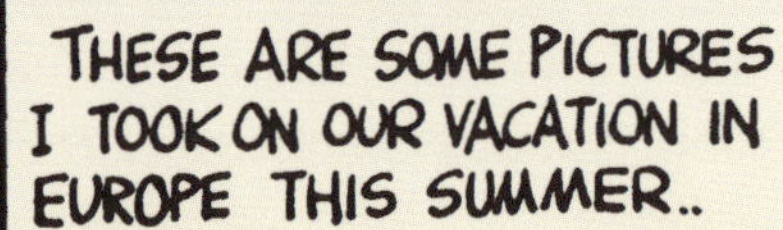
THESE ARE SOME PICTURES I TOOK ON OUR VACATION IN EUROPE THIS SUMMER..

HERE'S ONE OF BEETHOVEN'S HOUSE IN "BONN AM RHEIN"...

THIS IS A SCULPTURE WHICH STANDS IN THE LITTLE GARDEN JUST BEHIND THE HOUSE..

HERE I AM AGAIN POSING BY THE HOUSE
11-16

WILL THESE PICTURES BE WORTH A LOT OF MONEY SOMEDAY?

I DOUBT IT..

I DON'T SEE HOW ANYBODY CAN SAVE SOMETHING THAT WON'T BE WORTH A LOT OF MONEY SOMEDAY..
SCHULZ

SNOOPY!
PEANUTS
by CHARLES M. SCHULZ

WHERE **IS** THAT CRAZY DOG?

SNOOPY! SUPPERTIME!!

SNIF SNIF

GOOD GRIEF!

11-23
I'M GETTING TO BE LIKE A HOUSEWIFE... I HATE MEALTIME! I **HATE** IT!!

ALL RIGHT, IF YOU DON'T WANT YOUR SUPPER, I'LL GIVE IT TO THE CAT NEXT DOOR!!

SCHULZ

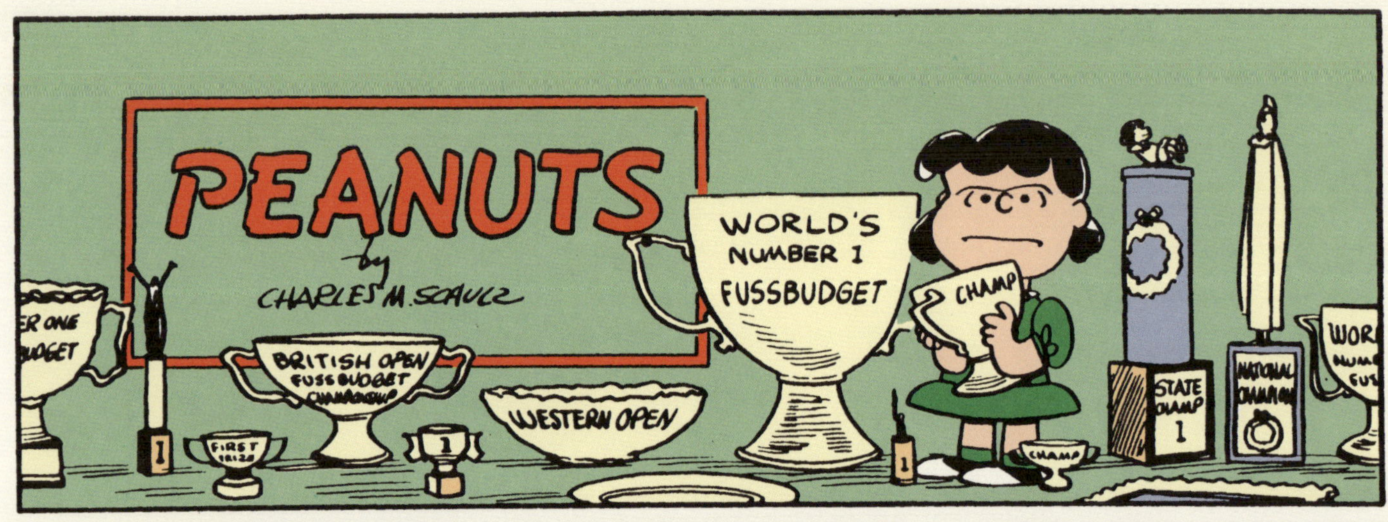
PEANUTS
by CHARLES M. SCHULZ
WORLD'S NUMBER 1 FUSSBUDGET
CHAMP
BRITISH OPEN FUSSBUDGET CHAMPIONSHIP
WESTERN OPEN
FIRST PRIZE
STATE CHAMP 1
NATIONAL CHAMPION

GIMME THAT BOOK! THAT'S MY BOOK!!

I DON'T WANNA WATCH THAT PROGRAM.. I WANNA WATCH MY PROGRAM!

ALL RIGHT, I'LL GO UPSTAIRS, AND LISTEN TO THE RADIO..

I DON'T WANNA LISTEN TO THAT PROGRAM... I WANNA LISTEN TO MY PROGRAM!!

ALL RIGHT... I'LL GO IN THE NEXT ROOM, AND PLAY A FEW RECORDS...

I DON'T WANNA LISTEN TO THOSE RECORDS.. I WANNA LISTEN TO MY RECORDS!

11-30
ALL RIGHT, I'LL GO OUTSIDE, AND LOOK AT THE STARS FOR A WHILE..
SCHULZ

I DON'T WANNA LOOK AT THOSE STARS..I WANNA LOOK AT MY...

SIGH

PEANUTS
by
CHARLES M. SCHULZ

CHARLIE BROWN, IF A STAR FELL DOWN HERE, WOULD YOU BE ALLOWED TO PUT IT IN A PAIL, AND TAKE IT HOME?

WELL, IN THE FIRST PLACE LINUS, A STAR IS PRETTY BIG.. YOU'D NEVER BE ABLE TO GET ONE IN A PAIL...
YOU WOULDN'T?

NOPE! I'M AFRAID NOT..

12-7

SCHULZ

PEANUTS
by SCHULZ

CLOMP!

12-14
WHEW
PUFF
PUFF

SCHULZ

PEANUTS
"WE ARE HERE TO TELL YOU OF A WONDROUS LIGHT"
I'M SUNK!

"A WONDROUS LIGHT THAT WAS A STAR"
I WONDER IF THERE'S ANY WAY I COULD GET OUT OF HERE...

"THE WISE MEN SAW THE STAR, AND FOLLOWED IT FROM AFAR.."
PSST... LUCY..

"THEY FOUND THE STABLE IN THE NIGHT BENEATH THE STAR SO BIG AND BRIGHT.."
WHAT'S THE MATTER?
I CAN'T REMEMBER MY PIECE!

"THE WISE-MEN LEFT THE PRESENTS THERE...GIFTS SO PRECIOUS AND SO RARE.."
WADDYA MEAN, YOU CAN'T REMEMBER IT?
I CAN'T REMEMBER IT!

"LOOK UP, LOOK UP, THE STAR STILL STANDS, SEEN BY MILLIONS IN MANY LANDS.."
YOU BETTER REMEMBER IT RIGHT NOW, YOU BLOCKHEAD, OR WHEN WE GET HOME, I'LL SLUG YOU A GOOD ONE!

"THE STAR THAT SHONE AT BETHLEHEM STILL SHINES FOR US TODAY!"
12-21

MERRY CHRISTMAS
THANK YOU..
SCHULZ

PEANUTS
by SCHULZ

?
SNAP!

YOU BROKE ALL MY CRAYONS IN HALF!

ARE YOU OUT OF YOUR MIND?
NO, I DON'T THINK SO...OF COURSE, I HAVEN'T TAKEN ANY ACTUAL INTELLIGENCE TESTS LATELY SO I..

YOU'RE GOING TO DRIVE ME CRAZY!!

HERE! NOW GET TO WORK!!!

12-28
HAVE YOU EVER TRIED TO GLUE CRAYONS TOGETHER?

PEANUTS
by SCHULZ
1-4
SCHULZ

 JANUARY 11, 1959

PEANUTS
by
CHARLES M. SCHULZ

1-18

SCHULZ

PEANUTS
by SCHULZ

CLOMP!

WHAM

WEAK ANKLES!
SCHULZ
1-25

PEANUTS
by
SCHULZ

I CAN'T STAND IT!

SCHULZ
2-1
WHAT'S THE MATTER? DON'T YOU **LIKE** CHRISTMAS CAROLS?

PEANUTS
by SCHULZ

CLOMP!

Hey! LET GO!! LET GO OF THAT MITTEN!

2-8
LET GO, I SAY!!

WOOP!

THEY SURE HAVE A LOT OF NEW THINGS THESE DAYS FOR DOGS TO WEAR IN COLD WEATHER..
2-8
SCHULZ

PEANUTS

BEAUTIFUL! JUST BEAUTIFUL!

YOU KNOW WHAT HE NEEDS? HE NEEDS SOME GLOVES!
AND AN OLD HAT! HOW ABOUT AN OLD HAT?

OUR SNOWMAN REMINDS ME OF SOME GREAT HISTORIC FIGURE!
UH HUH.. UNTOUCHED AND UNMARRED BY MODERN CIVILIZATION!

SCHULZ

PEANUTS
WHERE DID YOU FIND IT?
HE LEFT IT AT OUR HOUSE ONE DAY LAST SUMMER WHEN WE WERE ALL PLAYING UNDER THE SPRINKLER..

CAN YOU GET IT OVER YOUR HEAD?
IF HE CAN, I CAN!
?

LUCY'S PUTTING ON ONE OF CHARLIE BROWN'S T-SHIRTS..

LOOK! I'M CHARLIE BROWN!

NOBODY LIKES ME! EVERYBODY HATES ME! POOR, POOR ME!

I WISH I HAD A FRIEND! EVERYBODY HATES ME!! NOBODY LIKES ME!
HA HA HA HA HA HA HA HA HA HA HA HA HA HA

HEY! HERE COMES CHARLIE BROWN HIMSELF! OH, BOY, JUST WAIT 'TIL HE SEES LUCY!
THIS OUGHT TO BE GOOD!

!

WELL, HELLO THERE, CHARLIE BROWN, YOU BLOCKHEAD!!

SCHULZ
SIGH
HA HA HA HA HA HA HA HA HA HA HA HA HA

PEANUTS
by SCHULZ
RATS! THAT'S THE FOURTH TIME TODAY THE WIND HAS BLOWN OFF MY CAP!

WELL, AT LEAST IT'S A GOOD DAY FOR FLYING KITES...

WHOOPS! THERE IT GOES AGAIN!

I'LL GET IT, CHARLIE BROWN... YOU WATCH THE KITE!

THANK YOU... NOW YOU HOLD ON TO THE KITE UNTIL I START RUNNING WITH IT..
KITE FLYTE

RATS! I'M THE WORLD'S WORST KITE-FLYER!
HERE'S YOUR CAP... IT BLEW CLEAR ACROSS THE STREET!

WHOOPS!
THERE IT GOES AGAIN!

I HAVE A SUGGESTION TO MAKE, CHARLIE BROWN...

WHY DON'T YOU TRY WEARING THE KITE, AND FLYING YOUR CAP?
3-1
SCHULZ

MARCH 1, 1959

PEANUTS
by SCHULZ

I'LL PUT UP THE WICKETS, LINUS, AND YOU POUND IN THE STAKES...OKAY?
FINE.. I ALWAYS LIKE TO TACKLE A MAN'S JOB!

WHAP
WAP
WHAPPITY
WHAP

POW
POW
POW

OH, GOOD GRIEF!

?

3-8
SCHULZ

PEANUTS

SHEER JEALOUSY

BOOM!

SCHULZ

PEANUTS

THERE'S A LESSON TO BE LEARNED HERE SOMEWHERE, BUT I DON'T KNOW WHAT IT IS...
SCHULZ

PEANUTS
BOY, I FEEL SHARP TODAY..

JAB! JAB! JAB! POW! POW! POW!!

OKAY...ROUND ONE WILL START AS SOON AS THAT JET GOES OVER..

JET? WHAT JET?

3-29
WOP!

WOULD YOU LIKE TO SIGN A PETITION TO HAVE THE JETS MOVED AWAY FROM OUR CITY?
SCHULZ

1
3
3
1
PEANUTS
by SCHULZ

THUMP!
SNOOPY

SNOOPY

WUMP!

I'M A COLD-BLOODED KILLER!
4-5
SCHULZ

APRIL 12, 1959

PEANUTS
by SCHULZ

WHAT DO YOU HAVE THERE, CHARLIE BROWN?
I'VE WRITTEN A POEM..

REALLY? READ IT..
ALL RIGHT.. IT ISN'T VERY LONG..

SOME DAYS YOU THINK MAYBE YOU KNOW EVERYTHING...SOME DAYS YOU THINK MAYBE YOU DON'T KNOW ANYTHING... SOME DAYS YOU THINK YOU KNOW A FEW THINGS...SOME DAYS YOU DON'T EVEN KNOW HOW OLD YOU ARE.

THAT'S THE WORST POEM I'VE EVER HEARD!
4-19

A POEM IS SUPPOSED TO HAVE FEELING! YOUR POEM COULDN'T TOUCH ANYONE'S HEART! YOUR POEM COULDN'T MAKE ANYONE CRY! YOUR POEM COULDN'T..

WAAH!

SOME DAYS YOU THINK MAYBE YOU KNOW EVERYTHING...SOME DAYS YOU THINK MAYBE YOU..
SNIF
GOOD GRIEF!
SCHULZ

PEANUTS
by
SCHULZ

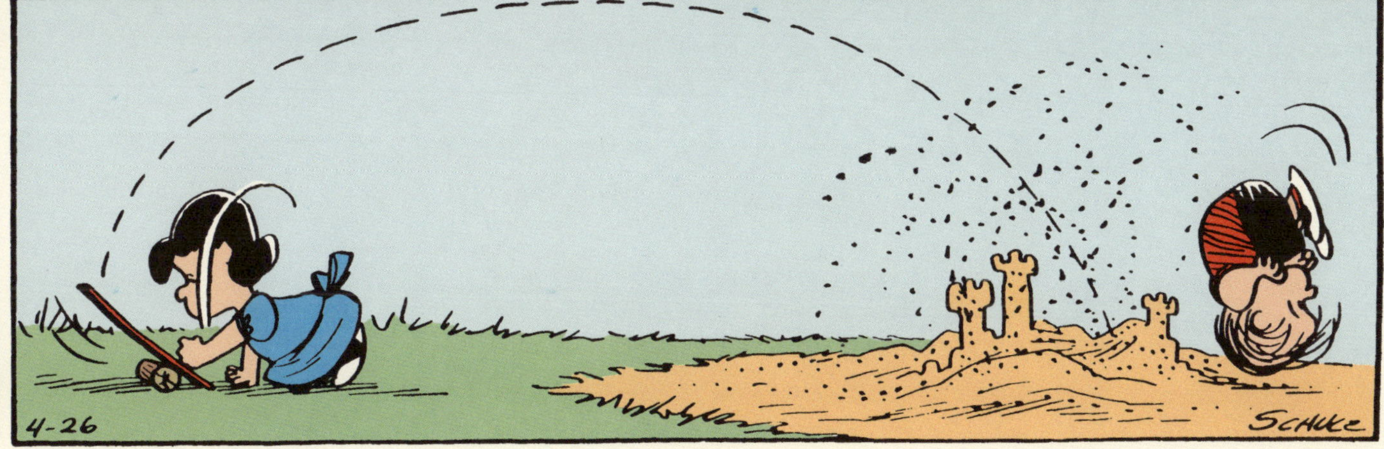
4-26
SCHULZ

PEANUTS
HEY, MANAGER..I WANNA TALK WITH YOU!

WHY DO I HAVE TO PLAY IN THE OUTFIELD ALL THE TIME? HUH?

WHY DON'T I EVER GET TO PLAY IN THE INFIELD?

HOW COME I HAVE TO PLAY IN THE OUTFIELD ALL THE TIME?

I'M A BORN INFIELDER! I SHOULDN'T BE STUCK OUT THERE ALL THE TIME

HOW COME I CAN'T EVER PLAY SOMETHING BESIDES OUTFIELD? HUH? HUH?

WHY SHOULD I HAVE TO PLAY IN THE OUTFIELD ALL THE TIME? WHY?

WHY SHOULDN'T I PLAY IN THE INFIELD NOW AND THEN? HUH?

HOW COME I HAVE TO PLAY IN THE OUTFIELD ALL THE TIME? HUH? HOW COME? HUH? HUH?

ALL RIGHT! I'LL LET YOU PLAY SHORTSTOP, BUT IF SOMEBODY HITS YOU A HOT ONE, DON'T COME CRYING TO ME!

POW!

LOOK AT ME..I'M AN OUTFIELDER!
SCHULZ

MAY 3, 1959

PEANUTS
by SCHULZ

HI..
HI..

WHAT ARE YOU DOING THERE? YOU'RE SUPPOSED TO COLOR THE SKY **BLUE**

BLUE? THE SKY ISN'T **ALL** BLUE!
IT ISN'T?

THE SKY IS MANY COLORS..THERE'S A LITTLE BIT OF YELLOW THERE, SOME WHITE, SOME PINK, SOME GREEN AND..
YOU'RE CRAZY!

WELL, GO ON OUTSIDE, AND LOOK FOR YOURSELF!

ALL RIGHT, I WILL!!

WOULDN'T YOU SAY THE SKY IS BLUE, CHARLIE BROWN?

NO, I SHOULD SAY THE SKY IS MANY COLORS..THERE'S A LITTLE BIT OF YELLOW THERE, SOME WHITE, SOME PINK, SOME GREEN AND..
5-10

I OUGHTA SLUG YOU A GOOD ONE!

I DON'T EVEN KNOW WHAT'S GOING ON!!
SCHULZ

PEANUTS
by SCHULZ

THE STARS ARE BEAUTIFUL, AREN'T THEY?
UH, HUH..

YOU KNOW WHAT I THINK?

I THINK THAT THERE MUST BE A TINY STAR OUT THERE THAT IS MY STAR..

AND, AS I AM ALONE HERE ON EARTH AMONG MILLIONS OF PEOPLE, THAT TINY STAR IS OUT THERE ALONE AMONG MILLIONS AND MILLIONS OF STARS!

DOES THAT MAKE ANY SENSE, LUCY? DO YOU THINK IT MEANS ANYTHING?
CERTAINLY..

IT MEANS YOU'RE CRACKING UP, CHARLIE BROWN!
SCHULZ
5-17

PEANUTS
by
SCHULZ

TUM DE DA.. DE DUM DE DA DE DUM DE DA

WHAM!

PERHAPS YOU SHOULD SEE A DOCTOR...
5-24
SCHULZ

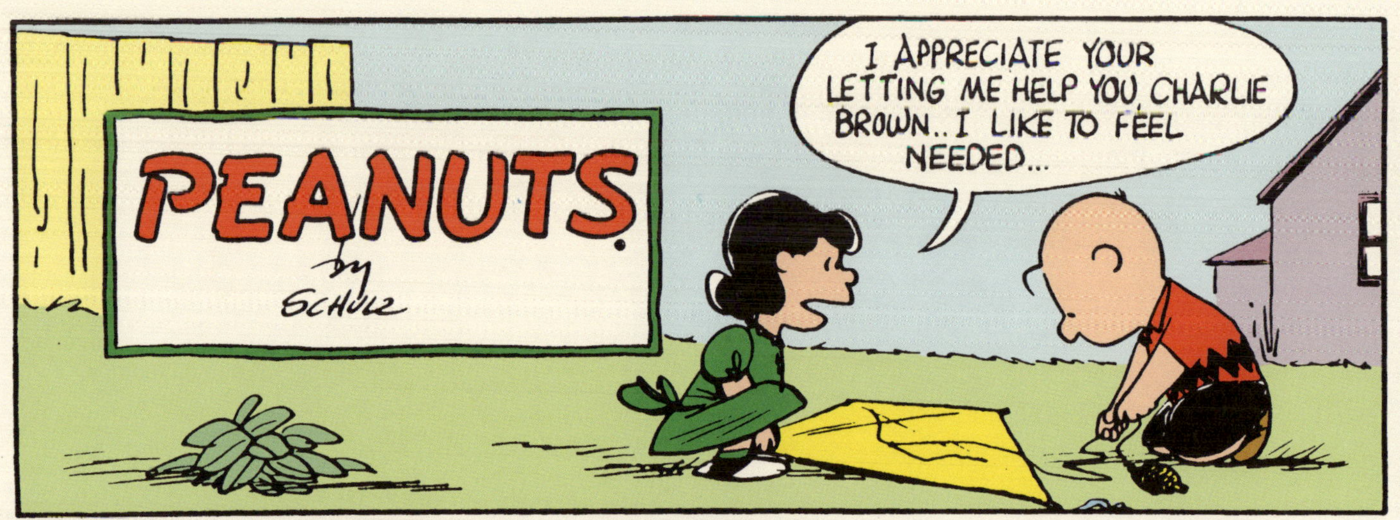
PEANUTS
by SCHULZ
I APPRECIATE YOUR LETTING ME HELP YOU, CHARLIE BROWN.. I LIKE TO FEEL NEEDED...

I'LL BET THIS KITE WILL FLY CLEAR UP TO THE CLOUDS!
WELL, WE'LL SEE...

OKAY... LET GO!

IT'S UP! IT'S UP! YOU GOT IT UP, CHARLIE BROWN!

YOU GOT IT UP WITH MY HELP! WILL YOU TELL EVERYBODY THAT I HELPED YOU, CHARLIE BROWN?

WILL YOU? WILL YOU TELL EVERYBODY THAT WE WERE A TEAM, CHARLIE BROWN? THAT WE WORKED TOGETHER? HUH? WILL YOU?

5-31

WHAM!

I DON'T KNOW YOU!
SCHULZ

PEANUTS
by SCHULZ
Allegro

BEETHOVEN! ALWAYS BEETHOVEN!

I'LL BET BEETHOVEN REALLY WASN'T SO GREAT! I'LL BET HE DIDN'T EVEN HAVE ANY FRIENDS!

WHAT DO YOU MEAN, HE DIDN'T HAVE ANY FRIENDS?
JUST WHAT I SAID!

YOU NEVER READ ABOUT HIM PLAYING GOLF WITH HIS FRIENDS, DO YOU? HUH? DO YOU?! IF HE HAD SO MANY FRIENDS, WHY DIDN'T HE PLAY GOLF WITH THEM?

PEOPLE AREN'T FRIENDS UNLESS THEY PLAY GOLF TOGETHER! DID YOU EVER HEAR OF BEETHOVEN PLAYING GOLF WITH HIS FRIENDS? NO, YOU DIDN'T!

I CAN'T STAND IT! I JUST CAN'T STAND IT!

6-7

I WONDER IF LEONARD BERNSTEIN PLAYS GOLF WITH HIS FRIENDS?
SCHULZ

PEANUTS
by SCHULZ
BOY, HAVE I GOT SOMETHING FOR YOU!

HOLD YOUR CHIN UP... THAT'S THE WAY..
?

THIS IS A LITTLE BELL FOR YOUR COLLAR, SNOOPY... IT'LL GIVE YOU REAL CLASS...

WALK AROUND A BIT... SEE HOW YOU LIKE IT..

tinkle
tinkle
tinkle

TINKLE
TINKLE
TINKLE

6-14
WELL, WHAT DO YOU THINK?

SCHULZ
MOO!

PEANUTS
by
CHARLES M SCHULZ
YAWN

CLOMP

WUMP!

?

6-21

POOR KID...HE MUST
HAVE LOW METABOLISM!
SCHULZ

JUNE 21, 1959

PEANUTS
by
SCHULZ

DON'T LET THAT DOG LICK OFF YOUR ICE-CREAM CONE!

ARE YOU CRAZY? DO YOU WANNA GET A BUNCH OF GERMS? WHAT'S THE MATTER WITH YOU ANYWAY?

YOU SURE DO SOME STUPID THINGS! GOOD GRIEF!!

NOW, GO ON HOME! EAT THAT ICE-CREAM CONE YOURSELF!

I'M LESS THAN HUMAN!
SNOOPY
6-28
SCHULZ

PEANUTS

DO YOU WANNA SEE A KID
WITH A GREAT THROWING ARM?

WOP!

SCHULZ

THERE'S A KID WITH A
GREAT THROWING ARM!

PEANUTS
by
SCHULZ
BOY, I CAN HARDLY WAIT TO GET INTO THAT WADING POOL!

LOOK OUT, GIRLS! HERE I COME!

STAY RIGHT WHERE YOU ARE, CHARLIE BROWN!
THERE'S NOT ENOUGH ROOM FOR YOU!

GO FIND YOUR OWN POOL!
THAT'S WHAT I SAY! GO FIND YOUR OWN POOL!

7-12

SIGH
SCHULZ

PEANUTS
MOON
RAINING
WINDOW
BRIN
PICNIC
WUN
TU
FINI
OTH

WHAT ARE YOU DOING, LINUS?
I'M MAKING MY OWN SET OF FLASHCARDS

THESE ARE JUST LIKE THE ONES THEY USE IN SCHOOL, AND THEY'RE A GREAT AID IN LEARNING TO READ..

LOOOK

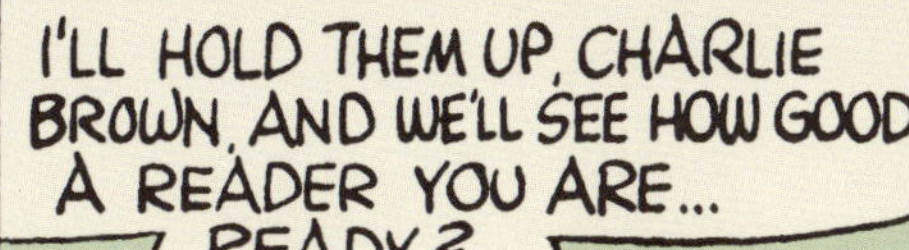
I'LL HOLD THEM UP, CHARLIE BROWN, AND WE'LL SEE HOW GOOD A READER YOU ARE... READY?

LOOOK
UH HUH!

VERY GOOD...NOW TRY THE NEXT ONE..
7-19

TAYBUL
GOOD.. AND THE NEXT?

KOW
VERY GOOD.. NOW LET'S GO A LITTLE FASTER..

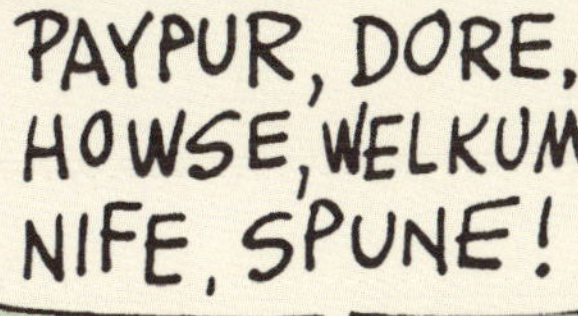
PAYPUR, DORE, HOWSE, WELKUM, NIFE, SPUNE!

EXCELLENT! DO YOU WANT TO RUN THROUGH THEM AGAIN?

NO, I THINK ONCE IS ENOUGH...

AWL THYS REEDING IS HARRD ONN MI EYYS!
SCHULZ

JULY 19, 1959

PEANUTS
by
SCHULZ

CLOMP

!
?

7-26
SCHULZ

YOU AND THAT STUPID BLANKET!
PEANUTS

HI, BOYS!

HOW DO YOU LIKE MY HAIR THIS WAY, CHARLIE BROWN?

IT LOOKS REAL NICE, VIOLET
I'M GLAD YOU LIKE IT... I WAS GETTING A LITTLE TIRED OF THAT PONY TAIL..

WELL, I THINK IT'S LOVELY THIS WAY... IT'S VERY BECOMING..
THANK YOU

"WELL, I THINK IT'S LOVELY THIS WAY... IT'S VERY BECOMING"

HA HA HA HA H
HA HA HA HA A
H HA HA H

SCHULZ

IN A WAY, THIS HAS BEEN A GOOD EXPERIENCE FOR ME. I HAVE LEARNED A LOT.
AS EVER,
CHARLIE BROWN

SCHULZ 8-9

AUGUST 16, 1959

PEANUTS
WHERE'S ALL YOUR STUFF, CHARLIE BROWN? WHERE'S YOUR GLOVE AND YOUR BAT AND EVERYTHING?
I CAN'T PLAY TODAY!

?

WADDYA MEAN, YOU CAN'T PLAY TODAY?!

JUST WHAT I SAID... I CAN'T PLAY TODAY! THERE'S SOMETHING ELSE I HAVE TO DO!!

BUT YOU'VE **GOTTA** PLAY, CHARLIE BROWN.. YOU'RE OUR **MANAGER**!

YOU MAY BE A **LOUSY** MANAGER, BUT YOU'RE STILL OUR MANAGER!
WE **NEED** YOU!
I CAN'T HELP IT...

YOU GOTTA PLAY, CHARLIE BROWN!
YOU GOTTA! YOU GOTTA!

I JUST DON'T UNDERSTAND IT!
I UNDER-STAND IT!
YOU UNDERSTAND IT? SINCE WHEN DID **YOU** BECOME SO UNDERSTANDING?

IT'S NOT A MATTER OF UNDERSTANDING

SIGH
IT'S SIMPLY THE AGE-OLD STORY!
SCHULZ

PEANUTS
by SCHULZ

I SURE LIKE CHARLIE BROWN'S LITTLE SISTER..

SOMEHOW I FEEL THAT SHE AND I HAVE SOMETHING IN COMMON..

I JUST CAN'T FIGURE OUT WHAT IT IS, THOUGH...

THAT'S IT!
8-30

SHE'S THE ONLY OTHER ONE AROUND HERE WHO KNOWS HOW TO WALK ON FOUR FEET!
SCHULZ

PEANUTS
by SCHULZ

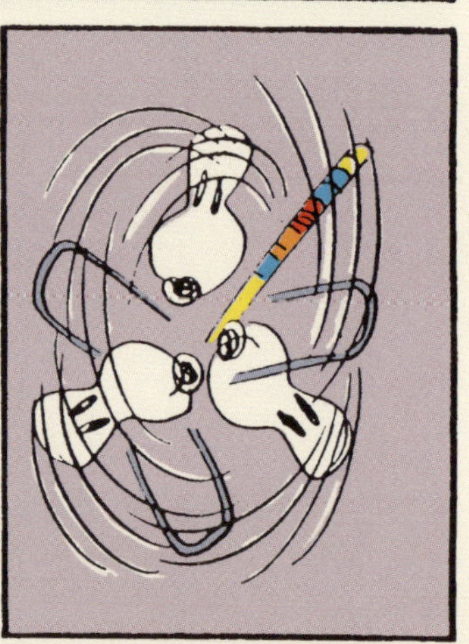

9-6

THUS ENDETH THE CROQUET GAME!
SCHULZ

PEANUTS
by SCHULZ
Z
?
A E

DOG food

OKAY, SNOOPY, YOUR SUPPER'S READY... COME AND GET IT!
MILK

OH, GOOD GRIEF!
Z

I SAID COME AND GET IT! I'M NOT GONNA WAIT AROUND ALL NIGHT! NOW, HURRY UP!!

Z

ALL RIGHT, IF YOU'RE NOT ANY MORE INTERESTED THAN THAT, I'LL TAKE IT OUT, AND GIVE IT TO THE NEIGHBOR'S CATS!!

9-13
SIGH
Z
SCHULZ

JUST LISTEN TO HER... I'M GLAD IT'S NOT **ME** SHE'S YELLING AT... I'D NEVER BE ABLE TO TAKE IT!

SHE'S GOOD ALL RIGHT... THERE'S NO DENYING THAT..

PEANUTS

PRETTY CLASSY!

HOW DO YOU LIKE MY NEW SHOES?
THEY'RE VERY NICE, LINUS..

!
SQUEAK
SQUEAK
SQUEAK
SQUEAK
SQUEAK

THEY KIND OF SQUEAK THOUGH, DON'T THEY?

WELL, MAYBE THEY'RE NOT PAID FOR... I'VE HEARD IT SAID THAT YOUR SHOES WILL ALWAYS SQUEAK UNTIL THEY'RE PAID FOR...

DO YOU MEAN TO TELL ME THAT JUST BECAUSE MY DAD HASN'T PAID HIS BILL, I HAVE TO WALK AROUND IN SQUEAKY SHOES?

I GUESS THAT'S RIGHT..
GOOD GRIEF!

IT'S ALWAYS THE CHILDREN WHO SUFFER FOR THE SINS OF THE MOTHER AND FATHER!
SCHULZ

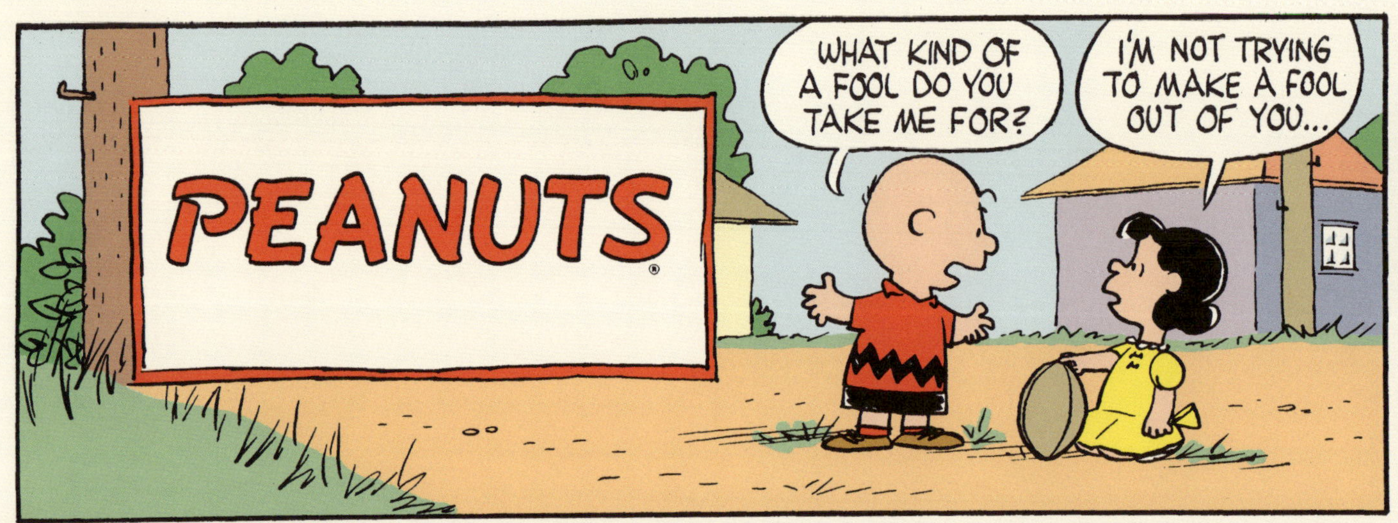
PEANUTS
WHAT KIND OF A FOOL DO YOU TAKE ME FOR?
I'M NOT TRYING TO MAKE A FOOL OUT OF YOU...

OH, YEAH?

THE WHOLE TROUBLE WITH YOU IS YOU DON'T TRUST ANYONE!

LOOK...EVERY YEAR YOU PULL THE SAME TRICK ON ME...YOU SAY YOU'RE GOING TO HOLD THE BALL WHILE I KICK IT, BUT YOU NEVER DO!

YOU ALWAYS PULL IT AWAY, AND I LAND FLAT ON MY BACK! EVERY YEAR YOU PULL THE SAME TRICK! **EVERY SINGLE YEAR!**

LISTEN, CHARLIE BROWN, IF YOU'RE GOING TO GET ALONG IN THIS WORLD, YOU HAVE TO LEARN TO BE **TRUSTING**...

ANYONE CAN TRUST SOMEONE WHO'S TRUSTWORTHY... I'M GIVING YOU A CHANCE TO LEARN TO TRUST SOMEONE WHO IS **NOT** TRUSTWORTHY!

YOU'RE RIGHT..I'VE GOT TO LEARN TO BE MORE TRUSTING...YOU HOLD THE BALL, AND I'LL KICK IT...

SHE DID IT AGAIN!

WHAM!

SEE YOU HERE AGAIN NEXT YEAR?
SCHULZ

PEANUTS
Bread

CHOMP CHOMP
CHOMP CHOMP CHOMP

CHOMP CHOMP
HANDS ARE FASCINATING THINGS!

I LIKE MY HANDS..I THINK I HAVE NICE HANDS...

MY HANDS SEEM TO HAVE A LOT OF CHARACTER...

THESE ARE HANDS WHICH MAY SOMEDAY ACCOMPLISH GREAT THINGS...THESE ARE HANDS WHICH MAY SOMEDAY DO MARVELOUS WORKS!

THEY MAY BUILD MIGHTY BRIDGES, OR HEAL THE SICK, OR HIT HOME-RUNS, OR WRITE SOUL-STIRRING NOVELS!

THESE ARE HANDS WHICH MAY SOMEDAY CHANGE THE COURSE OF DESTINY!

THEY'VE GOT JELLY ON THEM!

SCHULZ

PEANUTS
by
SCHULZ

10-18

IT ALWAYS COMES AS A SHOCK WHEN IT HAPPENS TO SOMEONE YOU KNOW...
SCHULZ

PEANUTS
by
SCHULZ

SMACK!
ZIP!

10-25

IF YOU CAN'T TRUST DOGS AND LITTLE BABIES, WHOM CAN YOU TRUST?
SCHULZ

PEANUTS
by SCHULZ
TRICKED! TRICKED BY A BABY AND A STUPID DOG!
SHE KISSES ME, AND HE GRABS THE BLANKET! I CAN'T STAND IT!
THE MORE I THINK ABOUT IT, THE MADDER I GET!

I GOTTA GET THAT BLANKET BACK!

WHO DID YOU SAY WAS HERE? DR. SPOCK? IN PERSON?

YOU SAY DR. SPOCK IS HERE IN PERSON JUST TO SEE US?

DID YOU SAY DR. SPOCK IS RIGHT HERE AT OUR FRONT DOOR? IN PERSON?

11-1

AND THAT NICE MAN FROM THE HUMANE SOCIETY? YOU SAY HE'S HERE, TOO?!

SCHULZ

PEANUTS
by
SCHULZ
SO THERE, TOO!!

NYAHH!!
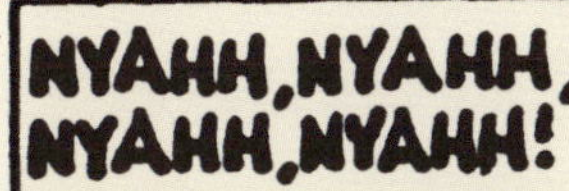
NYAHH, NYAHH, NYAHH, NYAHH!

IF YOU SAY THAT TO ME ONCE MORE, I'M GONNA SLUG YOU!

YOU CAN'T SLUG ME, LINUS, BECAUSE I'M A GIRL! NYAHH!!

WELL, BY GOLLY, I CAN SURE THROW A ROCK AT YOU! WHERE'S A ROCK? JUST LET ME FIND A GOOD ROCK...

HOLD ON THERE! YOU CAN'T THROW A ROCK AT A GIRL! ARE YOU CRAZY OR SOMETHING?

HOW ABOUT A TENNIS BALL? WHERE'S A TENNIS BALL? I'LL HIT HER WITH A TENNIS BALL! THAT'LL JUST STING A LITTLE..

NO, YOU CAN'T HIT HER WITH A TENNIS BALL EITHER!
HOW ABOUT A PING PONG BALL?

NO! YOU CAN'T HIT A GIRL WITH ANYTHING! YOU CAN'T EVEN THINK ABOUT HITTING A GIRL! THINKING ABOUT IT IS JUST AS BAD AS DOING IT!

CAN I SAY, "NYAHH" BACK AT HER?
NO, YOU CAN'T DO THAT EITHER!

HOW WOULD IT BE IF I SLUG YOU?
11-8
SCHULZ

PEANUTS
by SCHULZ
HERE COMES CHARLIE BROWN.. MAYBE HE'LL KNOW...

IT SURE LOOKS LIKE AN AIRPLANE TO ME...YOU KNOW HOW THEIR LIGHTS KIND OF BLINK ON AND OFF...

IS THAT AN AIRPLANE UP THERE, CHARLIE BROWN, OR IS IT A STAR?

I THINK MAYBE IT'S A STAR... OF COURSE, IT COULD BE A PLANET OR MAYBE EVEN A SPUTNIK...

I NEVER THOUGHT ABOUT. THAT... IT COULD BE A SPUTNIK, COULDN'T IT? I WONDER...

WELL, WE'LL NEVER FIND OUT BY STANDING HERE...THAT'S FOR SURE..
11-15

WHERE ARE **YOU** GOING?

I'M GONNA MOVE OVER HERE WHERE I CAN GET A CLOSER LOOK!
SCHULZ

I'LL LOSE MY MIND BEFORE THIS DAY IS OVER!
PEANUTS
TRY NOT TO THINK ABOUT IT...

I CAN'T HELP THINKING ABOUT IT!

I'M ONLY HUMAN!

OH, HOW I HATE MONDAYS!
RELAX!

HOW CAN I RELAX WITH MY BLANKET IN THE WASH? WHY DOES SHE HAVE TO WASH IT ANYWAY?! IT WASN'T VERY DIRTY!

I GOTTA HAVE THAT BLANKET!

I CAN'T BREATHE! THE WALLS ARE CLOSING IN ON ME! I'M GETTING WEAK! GASP-GASP-HELP ME, SOMEBODY! HELP ME!!!

AAAUGHH!

HOLD ON! HERE IT COMES!

FROM THE WASHER TO THE DRYER TO YOU!
SAVED!

SIGH!
I GUESS HE'LL BE ALL RIGHT NOW...

IN MEDICAL CIRCLES THAT IS KNOWN AS THE APPLICATION OF A SPIRITUAL TOURNIQUET!
SCHULZ

PEANUTS
by SCHULZ
HERE'S THE FIERCE MOUNTAIN LION SNEAKING THROUGH THE GRASS...

HERE'S THE AGILE MOUNTAIN LION BOUNDING THROUGH THE UNDERBRUSH.

HERE'S THE PROUD MOUNTAIN LION SITTING ATOP A ROCK..
11-29

SUDDENLY HE SEES AN APPROACHING FIGURE!

HE CROUCHES BEHIND THE ROCK...

HE LEAPS!!
GRAUGH!

RIP! SNARL! TEAR!

POUNCE POUNCE POUNCE POUNCE

SIGH

DEAR PENCIL PAL,
ON MY WAY HOME FROM SCHOOL TODAY I WAS ATTACKED BY A MOUNTAIN LION. I WAS NOT SERIOUSLY INJURED.
SCHULZ

PEANUTS
by
SCHULZ

YOU KNOW, I CAN'T POSSIBLY TELL YOU HOW SICK I GET OF SEEING YOU DRAG AROUND THAT STUPID BLANKET!

IT'S NOT STUPID... THIS BLANKET HAS MANY VERY PRACTICAL USES...

HA! THAT'S A LAUGH!
YOU JUST HAVE NO IMAGINATION, THAT'S ALL

I HAVE PLENTY IMAGINATION... IT DOESN'T TAKE ANY IMAGINATION TO SEE HE'S CRAZY!

OF ALL THE BROTHERS IN THE WORLD, I HAD TO GET HIM!

WELL, YOU'LL HAVE TO ADMIT HE'S DONE IT AGAIN!
HUH?

I SAID LINUS HAS DONE IT AGAIN..YOU'D BETTER GO SEE FOR YOURSELF...

?
12-6

SCHULZ

PEANUTS
by
SCHULZ
FIVE O'CLOCK...TIME TO FEED THE DOG..

DOG MEAL

OKAY, SNOOPY... HERE YOU ARE...

OH, IT'S SUPPERTIME! IT'S SUPPERTIME!

SUPPERTIME! SUPPERTIME! SUPPERTIME!!

HEY! CUT IT OUT NOW! WATCH WHAT YOU'RE DOING!

OH, IT'S SUPPERTIME! IT'S SUPPERTIME!!

YES, IT'S SUPPERTIME!

OH, YES, YES, YES, YES, IT'S SUPPERTIME! IT'S SUPPERTIME! IT'S...

ALL RIGHT, EAT!

GOOD GRIEF!

SO WHAT'S WRONG WITH MAKING MEALTIME A JOYOUS OCCASION?
SCHULZ

PEANUTS
by SCHULZ
YES, SIR... LONG PANTS SURE DO MAKE THE MAN!

WELL, HOW DO I LOOK?
FINE... IT'S THE FIRST TIME I'VE SEEN YOU IN A WHITE SHIRT IN SIX MONTHS!

NOW ARE YOU SURE YOU KNOW YOUR PIECE FOR THE CHRISTMAS PROGRAM?

I KNOW IT BACKWARDS AND FORWARDS AND SIDEWAYS AND UPSIDE DOWN! I COULD SAY IT IN MY SLEEP!

YEAH, WELL, I REMEMBER LAST YEAR.. YOU ALMOST GOOFED THE WHOLE PROGRAM!
WELL, THIS IS THIS YEAR, AND THIS YEAR I WON'T FORGET!

"AND THE ANGEL SAID UNTO THEM, FEAR NOT: FOR, BEHOLD, I BRING YOU GOOD TIDINGS OF GREAT JOY WHICH SHALL BE TO ALL PEOPLE."

SAY, THAT'S PRETTY GOOD..

I TOLD YOU I KNEW IT.. I HAVE A MEMORY LIKE THE PROVERBIAL ELEPHANT!

WELL, I'M GOING ON AHEAD TO THE CHURCH... I'LL SEE YOU THERE...
12-20

"...FOR, BEHOLD, I BRING YOU GOOD TIDINGS OF GREAT JOY WHICH SHALL BE TO ALL PEOPLE." WHAT A MEMORY!!!

WHAT IN THE WORLD? I THOUGHT YOU JUST LEFT?
I DID, BUT I CAME BACK..

I FORGOT WHERE THE CHURCH IS!
SCHULZ

PEANUTS
by SCHULZ
YOU'RE WEAK, YOU'RE WISHY-WASHY, YOU'RE DULL AND YOU'RE BORING!

I DON'T KNOW WHAT ELSE I CAN SAY...

THE WAY I SEE IT, CHARLIE BROWN, YOUR FAULTS SIMPLY OUTWEIGH YOUR VIRTUES!

I WISH THERE WERE SOME WAY TO DEMONSTRATE WHAT I MEAN..

I HAVE IT! I THINK I CAN GIVE YOU A GRAPHIC PRESENTATION WHICH WILL HELP YOU TO SEE YOURSELF AS YOU REALLY ARE!

THIS BOARD WILL REPRESENT AN EVENLY BALANCED PERSONALITY...NOW, ON ONE SIDE I'LL PLACE THIS PEBBLE WHICH REPRESENTS ALL OF YOUR VIRTUES...

ON THE OTHER SIDE I'LL PLACE THIS BOULDER WHICH REPRESENTS YOUR COUNTLESS FAULTS...NOW, WATCH WHAT HAPPENS...
12-27

WUMP!
BOING!

DON'T YOU THINK YOU'RE LUCKY TO HAVE ME AROUND TO POINT UP THESE THINGS IN SUCH A GRAPHIC MANNER?
SCHULZ

PEANUTS
by Schulz
I'M REALLY PERFORMING HIM A GREAT SERVICE..

I SORT OF WISH THAT SOMEONE HAD DONE SOMETHING LIKE THIS FOR ME WHEN I WAS YOUNG...

HERE, LINUS..LOOK WHAT I'VE DONE FOR YOU...

I'VE MADE UP A LIST OF NEW YEAR'S RESOLUTIONS THAT I FEEL YOU NEED DESPERATELY TO MAKE..

ACTUALLY THESE ARE REFORMS WHICH WILL HELP YOU TO BECOME A BETTER PERSON
WELL, HOW NICE!

THIS WAS VERY THOUGHTFUL OF YOU, LUCY... I SHALL TRY EARNESTLY TO IMPROVE MYSELF IN ALL THESE AREAS...

I'LL MAKE GOOD USE OF THIS LIST... I'LL TRY VERY HARD TO IMPROVE.. I REALLY WILL!

IN FACT, I THINK I'M GETTING BETTER ALREADY! LOOK AT ME... I'M IMPROVING!!

HAHAHA
HAHAHA

HAHAHAHAHAHA
HA
HAH
HA
HAH

1-3
REFORMERS HAVE A HARD LIFE!
SCHULZ

PEANUTS
by SCHULZ

CLOMP

WHEW!

ARE YOU CRAZY? IT'S **COLD** OUTSIDE! YOU COULD CATCH PNEUMONIA ROLLING AROUND OUT THERE IN THE SNOW!
1-10

THE STRUGGLE FOR SECURITY KNOWS NO SEASON!
SCHULZ

PEANUTS

I'M GOING HOME TO EAT LUNCH, SNOOPY, AND I WANT YOU TO GUARD MY SNOWMAN.. DON'T LET ANYONE HARM IT!

ONE THING I'M GOOD AT IS GUARDING THINGS! IT'S A POINT OF DISTINCTION WITH MY PARTICULAR BREED!

I'LL GUARD THIS SNOWMAN AGAINST ENEMIES FROM THE NORTH, SOUTH, EAST AND WEST! I'LL GUARD THIS SNOWMAN AGAINST ENEMIES FROM BELOW AND FROM...

........above..........

YOU JUST CAN'T DO **ANYTHING**, CAN YOU?
SCHULZ

PEANUTS
by SCHULZ
JANUARY ISN'T OVER YET...ACTUALLY, NINETEEN-SIXTY HAS JUST BEGUN!

I'VE GOT TO CONVINCE HIM! I'VE GOT TO!

LINUS, THERE'S STILL TIME FOR YOU TO MAKE A NEW YEAR'S RESOLUTION TO GIVE UP THAT BLANKET...

YOU KNOW, I THINK YOU'RE RIGHT! I THINK IF I'M EVER GOING TO GET RID OF IT, NOW IS THE TIME!
1-24

SO I'LL JUST THROW IT AWAY, AND BE DONE WITH IT ONCE AND FOR ALL!

NEVER BELIEVE ANYTHING I SAY!
SCHULZ

PEANUTS
by SCHULZ

HOLD IT!!

IS THIS ALL YOU HAVE TO DO? ARE YOU GOING TO SPEND THE WHOLE DAY SLIDING BACK AND FORTH ON A PIECE OF ICE?!

DO YOU THINK THESE DAYS WERE GIVEN TO YOU TO WASTE? DOESN'T LIFE MEAN MORE TO YOU THAN THIS?!

1-31
SCHULZ

PEANUTS
by SCHULZ

ALL RIGHT, YOU'VE WATCHED THAT PROGRAM LONG ENOUGH...NOW, I WANT TO WATCH MY PROGRAM!
CLICK

AAUGH!

I CAN'T STAND IT!

2-7
SHE'S GOING TO DRIVE ME CRAZY!

HOW CAN I LIVE WITH A SISTER LIKE THAT?!

I CAN'T STAND IT! I JUST CAN'T STAND IT!!!

RAUGHRGH!
RIP!
RIP!

GOOD GRIEF....

SHE HATH CAUSED ME TO REND MY GARMENT!
SCHULZ

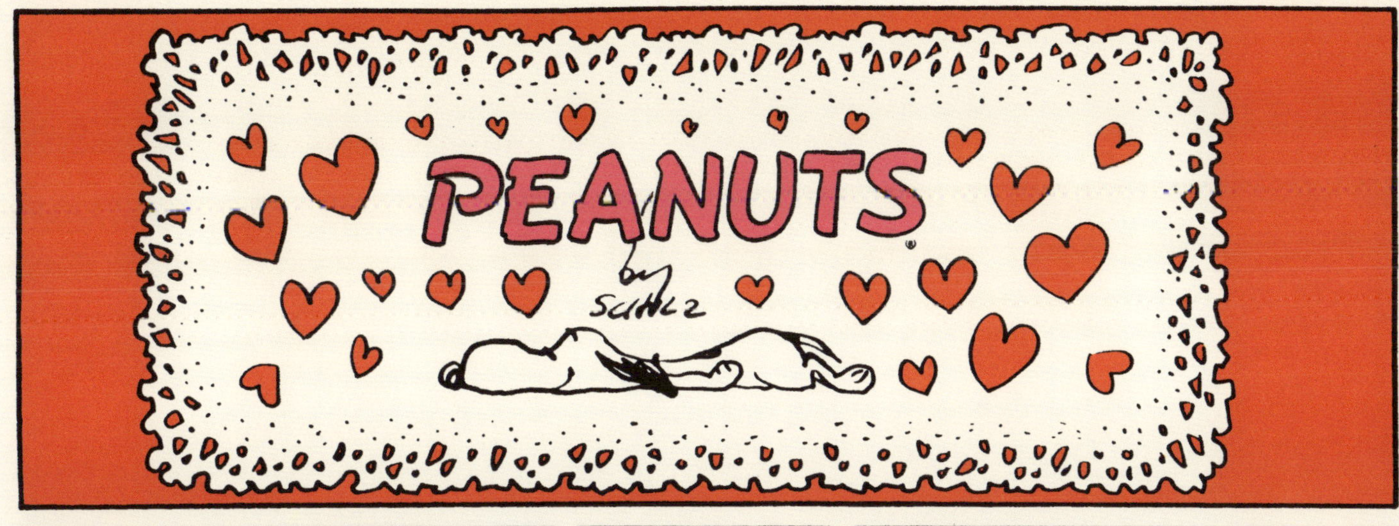
PEANUTS
by SCHULZ

I CAN'T STAND IT!

LOOK AT 'EM ALL LAUGHING AND ENJOYING THEMSELVES WITH THEIR VALENTINES!

I SENT EVERYONE I KNOW A VALENTINE, BUT DID I GET ANY IN RETURN? NO! NOT A SINGLE ONE!

EVERYBODY GETS VALENTINES EXCEPT ME! NOBODY LIKES ME!

LOOK AT 'EM! THEY ALL GOT VALENTINES! EVERYBODY GOT VALENTINES EXCEPT ME!

EVEN "PIG-PEN" GETS VALENTINES...
2-14

BUT DO I? NO!

I GET AS MANY VALENTINES AS A DOG!!

!

SIGH
SCHULZ

PEANUTS
by SCHULZ
YOU'LL NEVER MAKE IT! YOU'LL FREEZE TO DEATH!

DON'T TRY IT, CHARLIE BROWN! DON'T TRY IT!!

HE'S PERSISTENT, I'LL SAY THAT FOR HIM!

HE JUST NEVER GIVES UP...

OF COURSE, I'M NOT SO SURE IF THAT'S ALWAYS A GOOD WAY TO BE...

OH, OH... IT LOOKS LIKE HE'S GIVING UP... HE IS! HE'S COMING IN!

I'D BETTER OPEN THE DOOR FOR HIM.. HE MAY NEED HELP...

Brrrr!

2-21
YOU WERE RIGHT.. IT'S TOO COLD OUT TO FLY A KITE!
SCHULZ

PEANUTS
by SCHULZ
GUESS WHAT, LUCY...

I'VE FINALLY GOT A HOBBY!
YEAH, I'LL BET!

I'M STARTING A SNOWFLAKE COLLECTION..I'VE GOT SOME REAL PRETTY ONES IN THIS BOX...

YOU CAN'T KEEP SNOWFLAKES IN A BOX, YOU DUMMY!
YOU CAN'T?

2-28

I THOUGHT ABOUT WHAT YOU SAID...YOU KNOW, ABOUT NOT KEEPING SNOWFLAKES IN A BOX...

YOU'LL BE GLAD TO KNOW I SET THEM ALL FREE!
SCHULZ

PEANUTS
by
SCHULZ
ALL RIGHT...HERE!

YEAH, I MIGHT HAVE KNOWN THAT WOULDN'T SATISFY YOU!

GOOD GRIEF! CAN'T I EVER EAT ANYTHING IN PEACE?!

WHY DO YOU HAVE TO HANG AROUND ALL THE TIME ?!!

CAN'T YOU LEAVE A PERSON ALONE FOR EVEN ONE MINUTE?!!!

TICK
TICK
TICK

TICK
TICK
TICK

TICK
TICK
TICK

3-6
I CAN'T STAND IT!
SCHULZ

RUN, BOY! RUN!
PEANUTS
by SCHULZ

KEEP THOSE FEET MOVING!
LET OUT SOME MORE STRING!

KEEP GOING! KEEP GOING!

YOU GOT IT UP, CHARLIE BROWN! YOU GOT IT UP!

IT'S FLYING! IT'S FLYING!

IT'S...

BOOM!

3-13

THAT'S THE FIRST TIME I'VE EVER SEEN A KITE EXPLODE!
SCHULZ

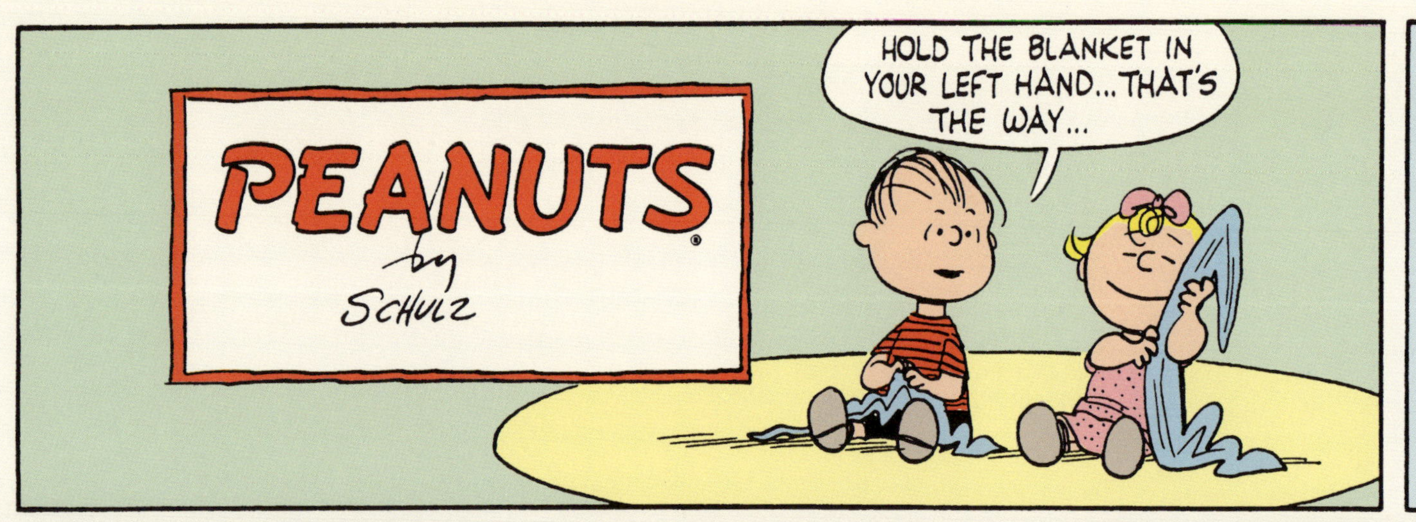
PEANUTS
by SCHULZ
HOLD THE BLANKET IN YOUR LEFT HAND...THAT'S THE WAY...

NOW THE THUMB...

WHAT IN THE WORLD IS GOING ON HERE?!

LOOK, LINUS, YOU'RE NOT GONNA TEACH ANY SISTER OF MINE TO SIT AROUND HOLDING A BLANKET!

JUST BECAUSE YOU NEED A CRUTCH, IT DOESN'T MEAN SHE DOES!

OF ALL THE STUPID HABITS, THAT BLANKET IS THE STUPIDEST! AND THAT'S ALL IT IS, JUST A HABIT! A STUPID HABIT!!

YOU'RE NOT GOING TO TEACH HER TO USE A BLANKET FOR SECURITY OR FOR HAPPINESS OR FOR ANYTHING! SALLY IS GOING TO USE HER OWN WILL-POWER TO GROW FROM A BABY TO A WELL-ADJUSTED CHILD!!!!

LIKE HER BROTHER?

3-20
SCHULZ
SIGH

IT'S THE SPIRIT OF THE TEAM THAT COUNTS! THE **INTEREST** THAT THE PLAYERS SHOW IN THEIR TEAM! AM I RIGHT?

I CAN'T TAKE IT... I'M GETTING SOAKED!
PEANUTS
THIS IS STUPID!

I'M GOING HOME!

LINUS! YOU'RE NOT LEAVING, TOO?!

OF COURSE, I'M LEAVING! YOU CAN'T HAVE BASEBALL PRACTICE IN THE RAIN!!

AND DON'T TELL ME IT'S GONNA CLEAR UP BECAUSE IT ISN'T!!!

YOU'RE LOSING YOUR MIND, CHARLIE BROWN, THAT'S WHAT'S HAPPENING TO YOU!

ANYONE WHO HASN'T GOT SENSE ENOUGH TO GET IN OUT OF THE RAIN IS CRAZY!

YOU'RE A FANATIC, AND YOU'RE LOSING YOUR MIND!!

IT'S RAINING HARDER EVERY MINUTE, AND YOU WANT TO STAND OUT HERE, AND PLAY BASEBALL!

WELL, I SAY YOU'RE CRAZY, CHARLIE BROWN! I SAY...

CHARLIE BROWN?

CHARLIE BROWN?

HE SHOULDN'T HAVE LEFT... IT LOOKS LIKE IT MAY CLEAR UP...

PEANUTS
by SCHULZ
WELL, LET'S SEE... CLIP-BOARD, PAPER, PENCIL... I GUESS I'M ALL SET...

THAT'S THE OL' STRETCH, SHERMY... YOU'RE GOING TO BE A GREAT FIRST BASEMAN!
THANK YOU, CHARLIE BROWN..

LET'S TRY TO MOVE IN A LITTLE FASTER ON THOSE GROUND BALLS, LINUS...
I'LL DO MY BEST, CHARLIE BROWN...

IF THE SUN BOTHERS YOU HERE IN LEFT FIELD, PATTY, WE'LL TRY TO GET YOU SOME DARK GLASSES...
OKAY, CHARLIE BROWN

WELL, HOW'RE THINGS AROUND SECOND BASE, "PIG-PEN"?
OH, A LITTLE DUSTY, MAYBE, BUT YOU KNOW ME... THAT'S RIGHT DOWN MY ALLEY...

ARE YOU MANAGING A BASEBALL TEAM OR ARE YOU INSPECTING THE TROOPS?
4-10
SCHULZ

PEANUTS
by SCHULZ

SCHROEDER, IF I TOLD YOU THAT I HAD THE FEELING YOU AND I WOULD GET MARRIED SOMEDAY, WOULD YOU CHUCKLE LIGHTLY OR LAUGH LOUD AND LONG?

I DON'T KNOW...IT'S KIND OF HARD TO SAY OFFHAND...
4-17

SCHROEDER, I HAVE THE FEELING THAT YOU AND I WILL GET MARRIED SOMEDAY...

HA HAHA
HAHAHAHA

HOHOHOHO
HAHAHAHAHA

HE'D LAUGH LOUD AND LONG!
SCHULZ

PEANUTS
SCHROEDER STILL MAKES THE BEST CATCHER WE'VE EVER HAD, AND "PIG-PEN" DOES WELL AT THIRD BASE..

OUR OUTFIELD COULD BE BETTER, BUT IT'S THE BEST WE CAN DO, I GUESS...

WHAT I'M LOOKING FOR IS A GOOD SHORTSTOP-SECOND BASE COMBINATION... TWO GUYS WHO CAN REALLY WORK THOSE DOUBLE-PLAYS...

WHAP!

CLOMP!

PTUI!

I THINK I'VE FOUND IT!
SCHULZ

PEANUTS
by
SCHULZ

WHAM!

5-1

WHAT A STRUGGLE...IT TOOK ME FORTY-FIVE MINUTES TO LAND HIM!
SCHULZ

PEANUTS
?

SNOOPY
? ? ?

OKAY, CHARLIE BROWN...LET'S GIVE HIM THE OL' FAST ONE... LET'S THROW IT RIGHT BY HIM!

!

5-8

HUMPH

WELL, WHAT ELSE CAN WE USE FOR HOME PLATE?
SCHULZ

PEANUTS
by
SCHULZ

?
CRUNCH!
CHOMP!
CRUNCH!

WHAT IN THE WORLD ARE YOU EATING?

CRUNCH CHOMP CRUNCH
CHOMP CHOMP
SMACK

SUGAR LUMPS WITH HONEY!

5-15

CRUNCH CRUNCH
CHOMP CHOMP
CRUNCH
CHOMP
CHOMP

THEY'RE GOOD WITH CINNAMON, TOO!
SCHULZ

PEANUTS
by
SCHULZ

SKRITCH
SKRITCH
SKRITCH

SKRITCH SKRITCH
SKRITCH
SKRITCH
SKRITCH

SIGH

MMMMMM?

SKRITCH SKRITCH
SKRITCH SKRITCH

5-22
SIGH

SCHULZ
ENCORE!

PEANUTS
by
SCHULZ
DRUGS
CANDY
ICE CREAM

CHOMP CHOMP CHOMP

CHOMP CHOMP
CHOMP CHOMP

!

6-29

SIGH

SCHULZ

MY GOODNESS, CHARLIE BROWN...HAVE YOU FINISHED THAT WHOLE BAG OF CANDY ALREADY?
WELL, I DIDN'T EAT IT ALL MYSELF... I SHARED IT WITH A "SLEEP-RUNNER"!

PEANUTS
by SCHULZ
TYRANNOSAURUS REX! LIFE SIZE, FIFTY FEET LONG AND TWENTY FEET HIGH! WOW!
MODEL SIZE...SIXTEEN INCHES LONG AND TEN INCHES HIGH...

HE SURE HAD A LOT OF BONES...

A DINOSAUR SET! OH, BOY! MAY I HELP YOU PUT HIM TOGETHER, LUCY?
OH, I SUPPOSE SO...

THIS LOOKS REAL INTERESTING.. THERE'S SOMETHING ABOUT DINOSAURS THAT'S FASCINATING..
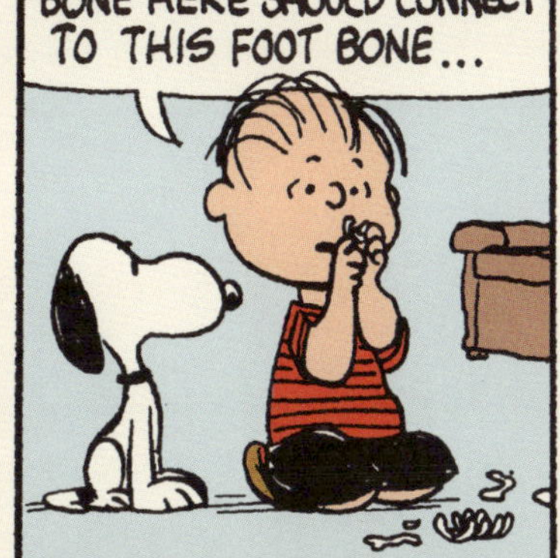
LET'S SEE NOW...THIS TOE BONE HERE SHOULD CONNECT TO THIS FOOT BONE...
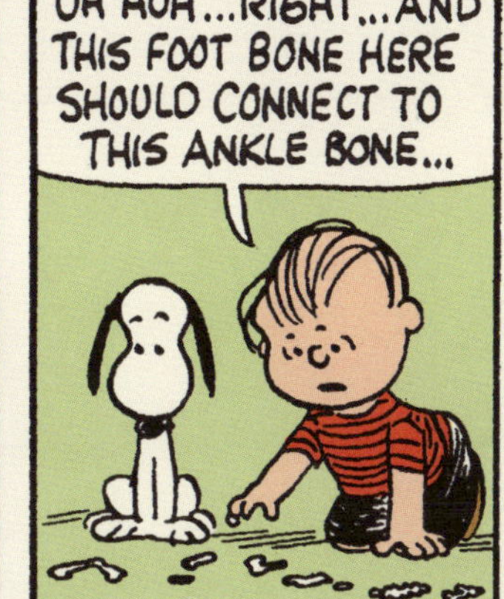
UH HUH...RIGHT...AND THIS FOOT BONE HERE SHOULD CONNECT TO THIS ANKLE BONE...

AND THE ANKLE BONE CONNECTS TO THE LEG BONE! RIGHT?

OH, THE ANKLE BONE CONNECTS TO THE LEG BONE...AND THE LEG BONE CONNECTS TO THE THIGH BONE!

THE THIGH BONE CONNECTS TO THE HIP BONE AND THE HIP BONE CONNECTS TO THE KNEE BONE
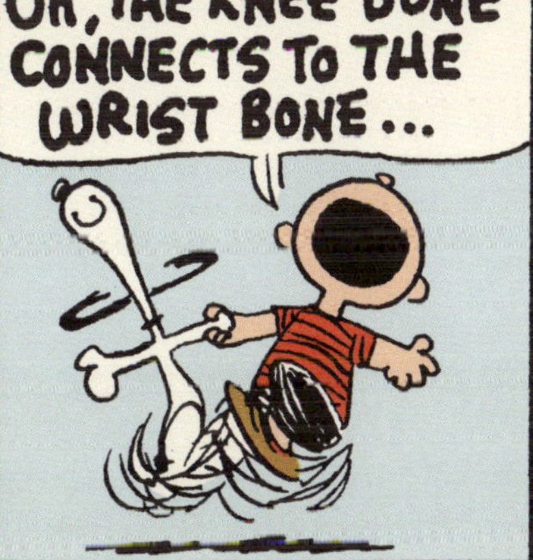
OH, THE KNEE BONE CONNECTS TO THE WRIST BONE...
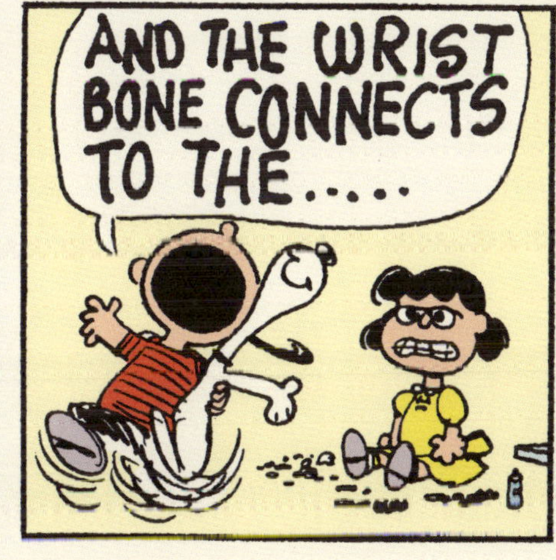
AND THE WRIST BONE CONNECTS TO THE.....

PEANUTS
by SCHULZ

?

6-12
WHEW

SCHULZ

PEANUTS
by
SCHULZ
Z
!
CHOW HOUND

Z

Z

Z

Z

Z

6-19

YOU DRIVE ME CRAZY!
SCHULZ

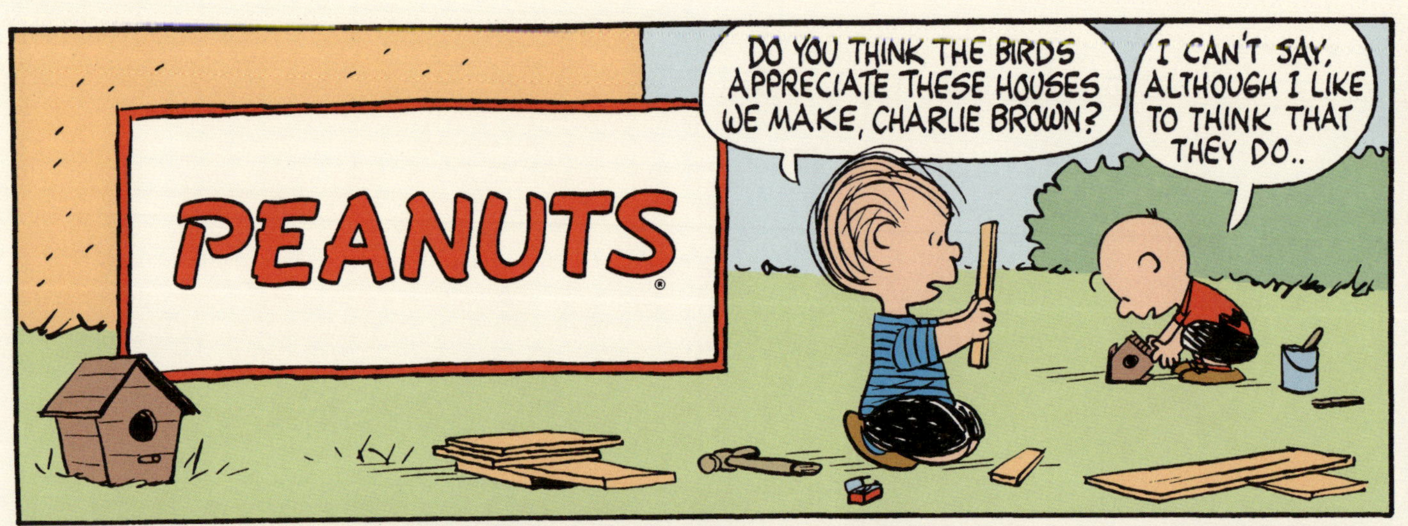
PEANUTS
DO YOU THINK THE BIRDS APPRECIATE THESE HOUSES WE MAKE, CHARLIE BROWN?
I CAN'T SAY, ALTHOUGH I LIKE TO THINK THAT THEY DO..

WE NEED SOME SMOOTHER BOARDS...A FEW OF THESE PIECES ARE PRETTY ROUGH...

AAUGH!
?

A SLIVER! A SLIVER! I GOT A SLIVER IN MY FINGER!!!

YOU'D BETTER GO HOME, AND HAVE YOUR MOTHER TAKE IT OUT..
IT'LL HURT! IT'LL HURT! SHE'LL STICK ME WITH A NEEDLE!! IT'LL HURT!!

OF COURSE, IT'LL HURT, BUT YOU DON'T WANT IT TO GET INFECTED, DO YOU?

I CAN'T STAND PAIN, CHARLIE BROWN!
SCHULZ

LOOK, DO WHAT I DO...WHILE YOUR MOTHER IS TRYING TO GET THE SLIVER OUT, YOU PRETEND YOU'RE BEING TORTURED BY PIRATES WHO WANT YOU TO TELL THEM WHERE THE GOLD IS BURIED

SEE HOW BRAVE YOU CAN BE..

AUGH

I TOLD THEM WHERE THE GOLD WAS BURIED!
SCHULZ

PEANUTS
by
SCHULZ

Z

Z
?
PARDON ME..

GOOD GRIEF!

THANK YOU VERY MUCH

7-3

IT JUST DOESN'T PAY TO LIVE TOO CLOSE TO THE BALL PARK!
SCHULZ

PEANUTS
YOU WANT ME TO LEAVE?
YOU THINK I WON'T LEAVE?
ALL RIGHT, I'LL LEAVE!
WELL, JUST WATCH ME!

I KNOW WHEN I'M NOT WANTED!

WHAT IN THE WORLD ARE YOU DOING?
PACKING! I'M GOING TO RUN AWAY FROM HOME!

HA! YOU BLOCKHEAD, YOU DON'T EVEN KNOW HOW TO RUN AWAY FROM HOME!!

YOU DON'T USE A SUITCASE!!! WHEN YOU RUN AWAY FROM HOME, YOU'RE SUPPOSED TO CARRY EVERYTHING ON THE END OF A STICK! THIS IS TRADITIONAL!

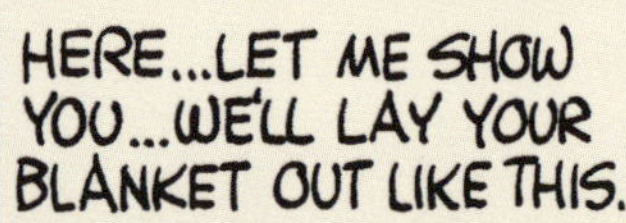
HERE...LET ME SHOW YOU...WE'LL LAY YOUR BLANKET OUT LIKE THIS..

THEN WE'LL WRAP ALL YOUR THINGS IN THE BLANKET, AND TIE IT TO A POLE...

THIS WAY YOU SORT OF PRESERVE THE TRADITIONAL PICTURE OF THE LITTLE BOY RUNNING AWAY FROM HOME

WHENEVER YOU SEE A PICTURE OF SOMEONE RUNNING AWAY FROM HOME, HE'S ALWAYS CARRYING HIS POSSESSIONS ON THE END OF A STICK..

SO LONG! HAVE A NICE TRIP!!

WRITE!

THERE HE GOES...THE LITTLE BOY RUNNING AWAY FROM HOME...

SCHULZ
I FEEL SOMEWHAT AKIN TO A FOOL!

PEANUTS
by
SCHULZ

LINUS! DON'T TELL ME YOU'RE RUNNING AWAY FROM HOME?!
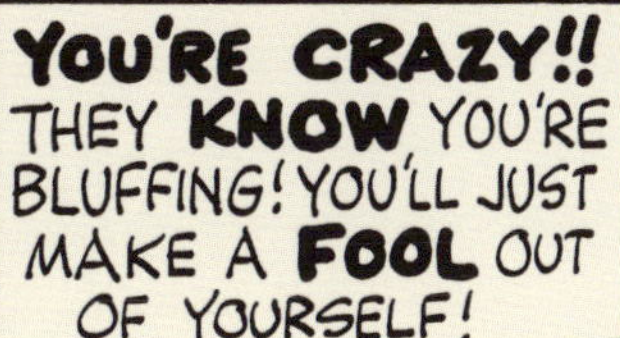
YOU'RE CRAZY!! THEY KNOW YOU'RE BLUFFING! YOU'LL JUST MAKE A FOOL OUT OF YOURSELF!

YOU'LL HAVE TO GO BACK HOME THIS EVENING, AND THEN YOU'LL HAVE TO LISTEN TO YOUR MOTHER AND DAD TELL EVERYONE ABOUT HOW YOU TRIED TO RUN AWAY, AND YOU WERE SO CUTE AND SO SERIOUS AND THEY'LL ALL LAUGH!

IT JUST DOESN'T DO ANY GOOD! THEY'RE WAY AHEAD OF YOU!

7-17

IN OTHER WORDS, YOU CAN'T FIGHT CITY HALL!
THAT'S RIGHT!

NOW, GO ON HOME, AND FORGET THE WHOLE THING..

WHEW I WAS SCARED TO DEATH SOMEONE WASN'T GOING TO COME ALONG AND TALK ME OUT OF IT!
SCHULZ

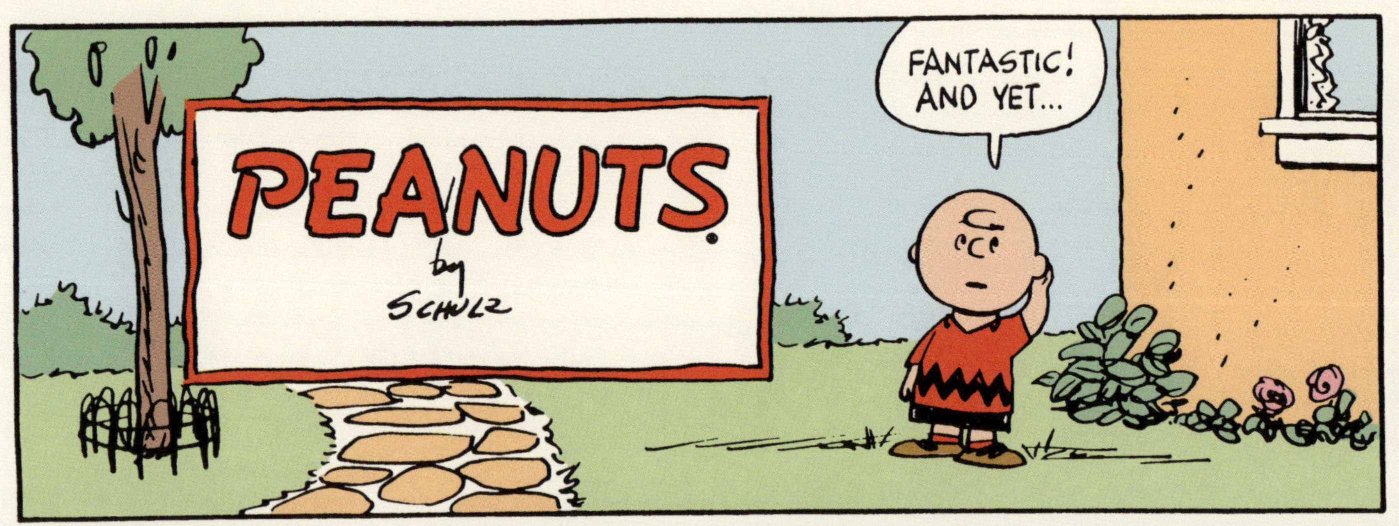
PEANUTS
by SCHULZ
FANTASTIC! AND YET...

SOMEHOW SHE DOESN'T SEEM QUITE HERSELF... JUST NOT THE SAME OL' LUCY...

I WANNA WATCH MY PROGRAM! I WANNA GO SWIMMING!

YOU SAID I COULD HAVE SOME ORANGE JUICE!

I DON'T WANT ORANGE JUICE! I WANT GRAPE JUICE!

rats

I'VE LOST IT, CHARLIE BROWN! I'M JUST NOT THE FUSSBUDGET I USED TO BE! I JUST CAN'T DO IT ANY MORE! I USED TO BE ABLE TO FUSS FOR HOURS...NOW I GET TIRED

I DON'T HAVE ANY VOLUME, I DON'T HAVE ANY TONE, I DON'T HAVE THE FEEL OF IT ANY MORE.. I'VE LOST IT! I'VE LOST IT! IT'S GONE!

IT'S KIND OF SAD TO SEE A GREAT TALENT LIKE THAT DETERIORATE
7-24

I GUESS THAT'S JUST ONE OF THOSE THINGS THAT HAPPEN, THOUGH.. ESPECIALLY IN A CREATIVE FIELD!

I DON'T WANNA TAKE A NAP! I WANNA PLAY OUTSIDE!!!

I GOT IT LICKED NOW, CHARLIE BROWN! I GOT IT LICKED!

FROM NOW ON I USE A 'THROAT-MIKE'!
SCHULZ

PEANUTS
by
SCHULZ

WHOMP!

WUMP
OOF

POW
7-31

WELL, HOW DID THE BOXING GO?
NOT SO GOOD... I GOT BEATEN..

REALLY? WHAT WAS IT THAT BEAT YOU? WAS IT A LEFT OR A RIGHT?

I DON'T KNOW...

WHEN YOU STOP TO THINK ABOUT IT, IT'S KIND OF HARD TO SAY!
SCHULZ

PEANUTS
by
SCHULZ

THIS IS TERRIBLE...I JUST CAN'T GET TO SLEEP!

THERE'S NOTHING WORSE THAN BEING TIRED, AND YET BEING...BEING....

8-7
Z

Z

BONG

SCHULZ
..WIDE AWAKE!

AREN'T THE CLOUDS BEAUTIFUL? THEY LOOK LIKE BIG BALLS OF COTTON...
PEANUTS
by SCHULZ

I COULD JUST LIE HERE ALL DAY, AND WATCH THEM DRIFT BY...

IF YOU USE YOUR IMAGINATION, YOU CAN SEE LOTS OF THINGS IN THE CLOUD FORMATIONS... WHAT DO YOU THINK YOU SEE, LINUS?

WELL, THOSE CLOUDS UP THERE LOOK TO ME LIKE THE MAP OF THE BRITISH HONDURAS ON THE CARIBBEAN..

THAT CLOUD UP THERE LOOKS A LITTLE LIKE THE PROFILE OF THOMAS EAKINS, THE FAMOUS PAINTER AND SCULPTOR...

AND THAT GROUP OF CLOUDS OVER THERE GIVES ME THE IMPRESSION OF THE STONING OF STEPHEN...I CAN SEE THE APOSTLE PAUL STANDING THERE TO ONE SIDE...

UH HUH...THAT'S VERY GOOD... WHAT DO **YOU** SEE IN THE CLOUDS, CHARLIE BROWN?
8-14

WELL, I WAS GOING TO SAY I SAW A DUCKY AND A HORSIE, BUT I CHANGED MY MIND!
SCHULZ

PEANUTS
OH, NO!

RATS! EVERY TIME YOU WANT TO DO SOMETHING, IT RAINS!

"RAIN, RAIN, GO AWAY... COME AGAIN SOME OTHER DAY!"

SLAM!

HIDE ME!
SCHULZ

PEANUTS
by SCHULZ
ALL RIGHT, TELL ME WHAT HAPPENED BEFORE MOM SEES US OUT HERE IN THE RAIN..

WELL, IT'S REALLY KIND OF SIMPLE...

ALL I DID WAS STAND OUT HERE LIKE THIS... AND THEN I SAID,..

"RAIN, RAIN, GO AWAY.. COME AGAIN SOME OTHER DAY!"

FRIGHTENING, ISN'T IT?
GOOD GRIEF!

I DIDN'T KNOW WHETHER I SHOULD CALL A DOCTOR OR A BOOKING AGENT..

DO YOU THINK I'M A DEMON? DO YOU THINK MAYBE THEY'LL STONE ME?

I DON'T WANNA BE STONED!!!

TAKE IT EASY... TAKE IT EASY... WE DON'T KNOW FOR SURE YET THAT IT WAS YOUR DOING..

IT'S ONLY HAPPENED TWICE..IF YOU CAN DO IT ONCE MORE, THEN WE'LL KNOW FOR SURE...WE'LL JUST HAVE TO WAIT NOW FOR IT TO START RAINING AGAIN...
8-28

I WONDER IF I CAN BE PATENTED?
SCHULZ

PEANUTS
by
SCHULZ
I WISH IT WOULD RAIN SO WE COULD GET THIS OVER WITH
I'M STILL AFRAID PEOPLE WILL THINK I'M SOME SORT OF A DEMON...I'D HATE THAT
DON'T EVEN THINK ABOUT IT

MAYBE THEY'LL FIND SOME VERY PRACTICAL USE FOR YOU...

WHAT IN THE WORLD ARE YOU TWO STANDING HERE FOR?
THIS IS A SCIENTIFIC EXPERIMENT, CHARLIE BROWN

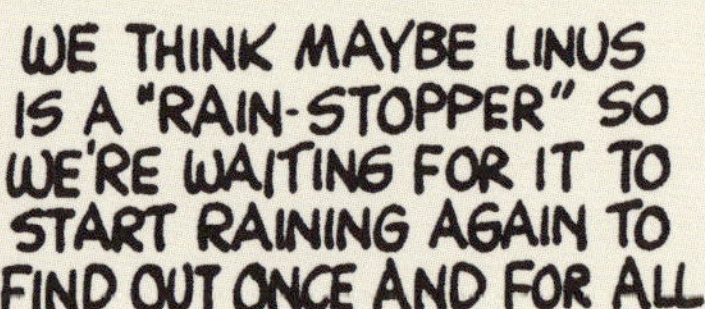
WE THINK MAYBE LINUS IS A "RAIN-STOPPER" SO WE'RE WAITING FOR IT TO START RAINING AGAIN TO FIND OUT ONCE AND FOR ALL

OH, OH! I FELT A DROP! IT'S STARTING TO RAIN! THIS IS IT!! THIS IS THE BIG SCIENTIFIC MOMENT!

9-4

GIVE IT ALL YOU'VE GOT, LINUS! MAKE IT STOP RAINING!

HURRY UP! SAY THE WORDS! MAKE IT STOP RAINING!
UH...

HURRY UP! SAY IT! SAY IT! SAY IT!!

GO GO TODAY, RAIN SOME WAY AGAIN SOME DAY!

OH, YOU BLOCKHEAD!

PEANUTS
by SCHULZ
HERE'S ONE END OF THE STRING RIGHT HERE...

I'LL BET HE NEVER GOT IT UP AT ALL...

SOMETIMES I THINK CHARLIE BROWN SHOULD GIVE UP TRYING TO FLY KITES...
HE SURE HAS AN AWFUL TIME...THIS IS THE WORST TANGLED KITE STRING I'VE EVER SEEN!

FANTASTIC!

HERE'S THE KITE IN THIS TREE...IT'S TORN PRACTICALLY TO SHREDS!

WHAT A SHAMBLES!
IT'S LIKE VIEWING THE BATTLEFIELD AFTER A GREAT STRUGGLE

I THINK I'LL TRY TO GET THIS MESS UNTANGLED...YOU GO SEE IF YOU CAN FIND CHARLIE BROWN...

9-11
DON'T BOTHER!
SCHULZ

PEANUTS
by
SCHULZ

WHAT ARE YOU FOLLOWING ME AROUND FOR?!

AM I SUPPOSED TO BE HONORED BY YOUR PRESENCE?

GO ON! GET OUT OF HERE! WHAT MAKES YOU THINK EVERYBODY WANTS YOU AROUND ALL THE TIME?!

SHE'S RIGHT...I MUST MAKE AN AWFUL NUISANCE OF MYSELF SOMETIMES...

SNOOPY!

OH, I'M SO GLAD TO SEE YOU! JUST KNOWING YOU'RE AROUND ALWAYS MAKES ME FEEL GOOD!

9-18

BLAH

SCHULZ

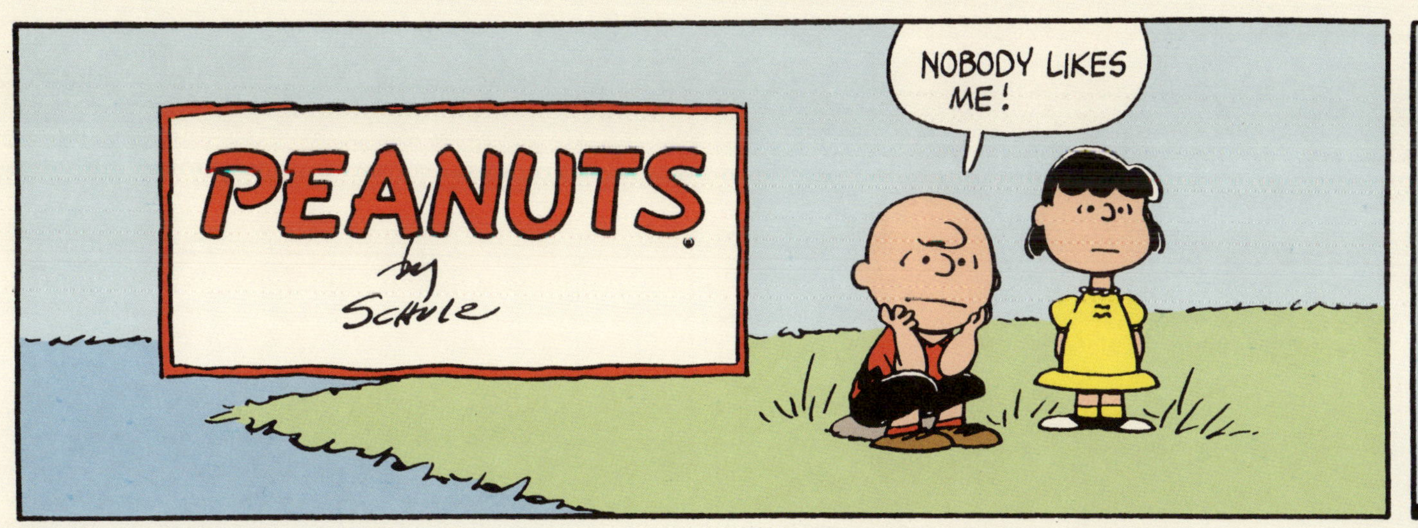
PEANUTS
by Schulz
NOBODY LIKES ME!

NOBODY **REALLY** LIKES ME!

ALL IT WOULD TAKE TO MAKE ME HAPPY IS TO HAVE SOMEONE SAY HE LIKES ME...

ARE YOU SURE?

OF COURSE, I'M SURE!
YOU MEAN YOU'D BE HAPPY IF SOMEONE MERELY SAID HE OR SHE LIKES YOU?

DO YOU MEAN TO TELL ME THAT SOMEONE HAS IT WITHIN HIS OR HER POWER TO MAKE YOU HAPPY MERELY BY DOING SUCH A SIMPLE THING?

YES! THAT'S EXACTLY WHAT I MEAN!
WELL, I DON'T THINK THAT'S ASKING TOO MUCH... I REALLY DON'T...

BUT YOU'RE SURE NOW? ALL YOU WANT IS TO HAVE SOMEONE SAY, "I LIKE YOU, CHARLIE BROWN."...

...AND THEN YOU'LL BE HAPPY?
AND THEN I'LL BE HAPPY!

9-25
I CAN'T DO IT!
SCHULZ

PEANUTS
by
SCHULZ
WHY DON'T YOU JUST KEEP QUIET? WHY DON'T YOU KEEP YOUR SILLY CHATTER TO YOURSELF? TAKE YOUR FOOLISH FACE SOMEPLACE ELSE!!

WHY DON'T YOU JUST LEAVE?!
GO ON!

GET OUT OF THIS HOUSE!

AND TAKE THIS STUPID BLANKET WITH YOU!

YOU CAN'T THROW ME OUT OF MY OWN HOUSE!

I LIVE HERE, TOO, YOU KNOW! YOU'LL NEVER GET AWAY WITH THIS! DO YOU HEAR ME?!!

SHE DRIVES ME CRAZY! I'M SO MAD I FEEL LIKE I'M GOING TO EXPLODE!!
10-2

I DON'T HAVE TO STAND FOR THIS! I DON'T HAVE TO TAKE THIS FROM HER!

I'M GOING TO TELL HER OFF LIKE SHE'S NEVER BEEN TOLD OFF BEFORE!

SLAM!

WELL?

I HOPE YOU DON'T GET ANYTHING YOU WANT FOR CHRISTMAS!
SCHULZ

PEANUTS
WHAT'S THAT?

WHAT'S WHAT?

I THOUGHT I HEARD A CAR DOOR SLAM!

IT'S DAD! HE'S BACKING THE CAR OUT OF THE GARAGE!

HEY, DAD! ARE YOU GOING TO THE STORE? WILL YOU BRING ME SOMETHING?

TELL HIM I WANT A COMIC BOOK!
LUCY WANTS A COMIC BOOK! AND I WANT A CANDY BAR!

I WANT A CANDY BAR, TOO!!
LUCY WANTS A CANDY BAR, TOO! AND I WANT A COMIC BOOK, TOO! AND CAN I HAVE A BOAT?

WILL YOU BRING ME A BOAT? OR A FOOTBALL?

WILL YOU BRING ME A CANDY BAR AND A COMIC BOOK AND A BOAT AND...

OH...

HE WAS JUST BACKING THE CAR INTO THE DRIVEWAY TO WASH IT!
SCHULZ

PEANUTS
by
SCHULZ
THERE! IS THAT ABOUT RIGHT?

IS THAT ABOUT RIGHT FOR WHAT?

I'LL HOLD THE BALL, CHARLIE BROWN, AND YOU KICK IT!

ARE YOU CRAZY?

YOU'LL JERK IT AWAY, AND I'LL BREAK MY NECK! DO YOU THINK YOU CAN FOOL ME WITH THE SAME STUPID TRICK YEAR AFTER YEAR AFTER YEAR?!

BUT THAT'S THE WHOLE IDEA, CHARLIE BROWN.. THE ODDS NOW ARE REALLY IN YOUR FAVOR!

ONE OF THESE TIMES I MAY NOT JERK THE BALL AWAY! ONE OF THESE TIMES I MAY ACTUALLY HOLD ON TO IT!

I NEVER THOUGHT OF IT THAT WAY...

OKAY...YOU HOLD THE BALL, AND I'LL COME RUNNING UP, AND KICK IT!

10-16

AAUGH!

WHAM

I'M SORRY...THIS WASN'T THE TIME!
SCHULZ

PEANUTS
by SCHULZ
..ANXIOUS CHILDREN WRITING THEIR LETTERS TO THE "GREAT PUMPKIN," GROUPS OF PEOPLE GETTING TOGETHER TO SING PUMPKIN CAROLS...IT'S WONDERFUL!

THERE'S SUCH A JOYOUS SPIRIT TO THIS SEASON!

YOU REALLY BELIEVE ALL OF THIS, DON'T YOU, LINUS?
WITH ALL MY HEART, CHARLIE BROWN..

I BELIEVE THAT ON HALLOWEEN NIGHT THE "GREAT PUMPKIN" RISES OUT OF THE PUMPKIN PATCH WITH HIS BIG BAG OF TOYS!

OH, WHAT A SIGHT THAT MUST BE TO BEHOLD!

THEN HE FLIES THROUGH THE AIR TO DELIVER THE TOYS TO ALL OF THE CHILDREN WHO HAVE BEEN GOOD

IF YOU'VE BEEN BAD DURING THE YEAR, YOU DON'T GET ANY TOYS!
THAT'S UNDER-STANDABLE

EXCUSE ME A MINUTE, CHARLIE BROWN..I WANT TO GO INTO THIS STORE..

THAT'S FUNNY..THEY SAID THEY DIDN'T HAVE ANY...IN FACT, THEY SAID THEY NEVER HEARD OF THEM...

NEVER HEARD OF WHAT?
PUMPKIN CARDS!

THAT'S VERY DISAPPOINTING...

I HAD PLANNED TO SPEND THIS EVENING ADDRESSING PUMPKIN CARDS!
10-23
SCHULZ

PEANUTS
IF ANYONE HAD TOLD ME I'D BE OUT CRAWLING AROUND AMONG A BUNCH OF PUMPKINS ON HALLOWEEN NIGHT, I'D HAVE SAID THEY WERE CRAZY!

THIS IS FAR ENOUGH..

JUST THINK, CHARLIE BROWN... WHEN THE "GREAT PUMPKIN" RISES OUT OF THE PUMPKIN PATCH, WE'LL BE HERE TO SEE HIM!

IT JUST OCCURRED TO ME THAT THERE MUST BE TEN MILLION PUMPKIN PATCHES IN THIS COUNTRY.. WHAT MAKES YOU THINK WE'RE IN THE RIGHT ONE?

JUST A FEELING I HAVE, CHARLIE BROWN, ALTHOUGH I THINK THIS MUST BE THE KIND OF PUMPKIN PATCH HE WOULD PREFER...

I DOUBT IF HE LIKES LARGE PUMPKIN PATCHES...THEY'RE TOO COMMERCIAL..HE LIKES SMALL HOMEY ONES...THEY'RE MORE SINCERE...
SOMEHOW I'VE NEVER THOUGHT OF A PUMPKIN PATCH AS BEING SINCERE...

THERE HE IS! THERE HE IS!

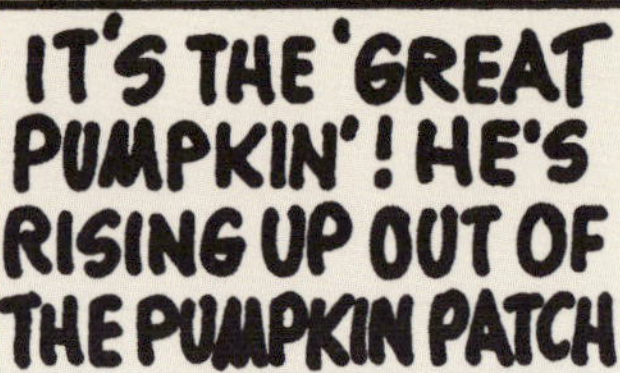
IT'S THE 'GREAT PUMPKIN'! HE'S RISING UP OUT OF THE PUMPKIN PATCH

OHHHOOO...
KLUNK

WHAT HAPPENED? DID I FAINT? WHAT DID HE LEAVE US? DID HE LEAVE US ANY TOYS?
NO TOYS... JUST A USED DOG...

HE MUST BE WELL ON HIS WAY BY THIS TIME.. HAPPY JOURNEY, O, GREAT PUMPKIN! HAPPY JOURNEY!
"USED DOG"! GOOD GRIEF!
SCHULZ

WHOOSH!

PEANUTS
POW
GOOD GRIEF!

POW!

SWISH!

OOF!

WHAM

DON'T TELL ME YOU GOT BEAT AGAIN?
YUP.. I ACHE ALL OVER..

WELL, IT SERVES YOU RIGHT.. BOXING IS A ROUGH SPORT...

THE ONLY PART THAT I THINK IS THRILLING IS WHEN THEY RAISE THE WINNER'S GLOVED-HAND IN VICTORY..
IN THIS CASE IT WOULD HAVE LOOKED PRETTY SILLY!
SCHULZ
11-6

PEANUTS
THIS IS GOING TO BE A NEW EXPERIENCE FOR ME...
I'VE NEVER FOUGHT A DOG WITH A BOXING GLOVE ON HIS NOSE BEFORE...

BOY, I FEEL SHARP TODAY! JAB! JAB! JAB! WAP!

ALL I CAN TELL YOU, CHARLIE BROWN, IS TO LOOK OUT FOR HIM... HE'S TRICKY..
I CAN BELIEVE THAT!

OKAY, FELLA, HERE WE GO! WATCH YOURSELF!

?

THE COBRA STRIKES!

POW!

DON'T FEEL BAD, CHARLIE BROWN... I'VE FOUGHT HIM TWICE, AND LOST BOTH TIMES...

I GUESS WE JUST CAN'T BEAT HIM..... I WONDER WHAT HAPPENS NOW?

I RETIRE UNDEFEATED... WHAT ELSE?
SCHULZ

PEANUTS
by
SCHULZ
THIS IS WHAT'S BEEN BEATING YOU IN ALL THOSE FIGHTS?

YOU LOOK RIDICULOUS!

WHOEVER HEARD OF FIGHTING A DOG WITH A BOXING GLOVE ON HIS NOSE?
HE'S THE CHAMP, LUCY...IF YOU'RE GOING TO BEAT HIM, YOU'RE GOING TO HAVE TO USE SOME STRATEGY...

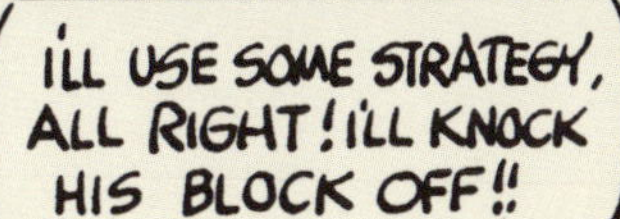
I'LL USE SOME STRATEGY, ALL RIGHT! I'LL KNOCK HIS BLOCK OFF!!

Y'GOTTA HIT ME FIRST, SISTER!

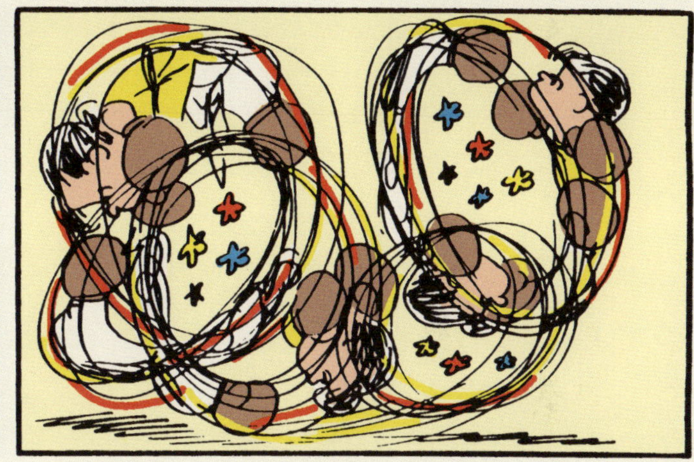

POW! WHAM!
11-20

BANG
WHAP! POW!
SOCKO!
OUCH! OOF!
LEGGO!
YIPE!

SCHULZ

 NOVEMBER 27, 1960

PEANUTS
by SCHULZ

DON'T BUG ME, DOG!
12-4

* SIGH *
SCHULZ

 DECEMBER 11, 1960

PEANUTS
"AND IT CAME TO PASS IN THOSE DAYS, THAT THERE WENT OUT A...A...??? "

RATS!

HOW CAN A PERSON LOOK FORWARD TO CHRISTMAS WHEN HE KNOWS HE HAS TO MEMORIZE A PIECE FOR A CHRISTMAS PROGRAM?

"AND IT CAME TO PASS THAT...THAT... IN THOSE DAYS THAT AUGUSTUS CAESAR, I MEAN CAESAR AUGUSTUS, SENT...SENT...???? "

I CAN'T DO IT! I CAN'T! I CAN'T!

I'LL NEVER BE ABLE TO MEMORIZE THAT PIECE! NEVER!!

I'M DOOMED!

?

OH, HI, CHARLIE BROWN.. SAY, HOW ARE **YOU** COMING ALONG ON YOUR PIECE FOR THE CHRISTMAS PROGRAM?

YOU KNOW, IF NONE OF US LEARN OUR PIECES, THERE WON'T **BE** ANY PROGRAM, WILL THERE? IF NONE OF US ARE ABLE TO MEMORIZE OUR PIECES, THEY...

"AND THERE WERE IN THE SAME COUNTRY SHEPHERDS ABIDING IN THE FIELD, KEEPING WATCH OVER THEIR FLOCK BY NIGHT."

THIS IS GOING TO BE A BLACK CHRISTMAS...
SCHULZ

PEANUTS
I'M NO PUBLIC SPEAKER...I'M NO PERFORMER.. WHY DO THEY HAVE TO HAVE THESE CHRISTMAS PROGRAMS?

THIS IS RUINING MY WHOLE CHRISTMAS!

I CAN'T DO IT! I CAN'T! I CAN'T REMEMBER A THING! I CAN'T! I CAN'T!

YOU'RE ON!

GOOD GRIEF!

"And it came to pass in those days, that there went out a decree from Caesar Augustus, that all the world should be taxed."

I DID IT! I DID IT! I SAID MY PIECE! I SAID IT! I SAID IT!!

HOW ABOUT THAT? BOY, WHAT A RELIEF! I DON'T WANT TO HAVE TO GO THROUGH THAT AGAIN AS LONG AS I LIVE!

IT'S ALL OVER, AND I DID IT! WHAT A RELIEF! BOY, OH, BOY! I CAN'T BELIEVE IT! IT'S ALL OVER, AND I DID IT!

WHAT'S THIS?
THIS IS THE PIECE YOU'RE GOING TO HAVE TO LEARN FOR THE NEW YEAR'S PROGRAM...

AAUGH!
SCHULZ

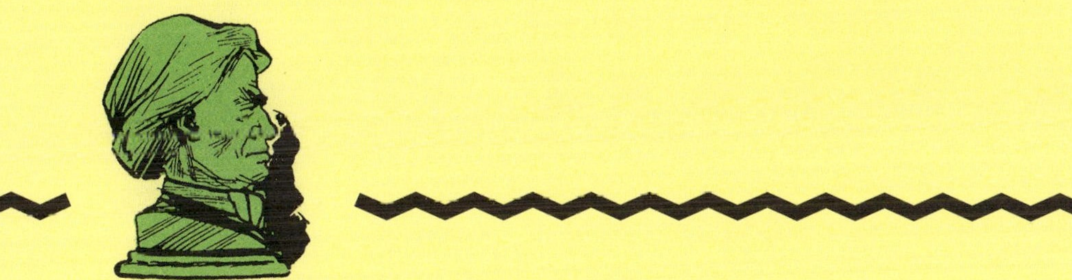

Charles M. Schulz was born November 26, 1922, in Minneapolis. His destiny was foreshadowed when an uncle gave him, at the age of two days, the nickname "Sparky" (after the racehorse Spark Plug in the newspaper strip *Barney Google*).

Schulz grew up in St. Paul. By all accounts, he led an unremarkable, albeit sheltered, childhood. He was an only child, close to both parents. His eventual career path was nurtured by his father, who bought four Sunday papers every week — just for the comics.

An outstanding student, he skipped two grades early on, but began to flounder in high school — perhaps not so coincidentally at the same time kids are going through their cruelest, most status-conscious period of socialization. The pain, bitterness, insecurity, and failures chronicled in *Peanuts* appear to have originated from this period of Schulz's life.

Although Schulz enjoyed sports, he also found refuge in solitary activities: reading, drawing, and watching movies. He bought comic books and Big Little Books, pored over the newspaper strips, and copied his favorites — *Buck Rogers*, the Walt Disney characters, *Popeye, Tim Tyler's Luck*. He quickly became a connoisseur; his heroes were Milton Caniff, Roy Crane, Hal Foster, and Alex Raymond.

In his senior year in high school, his mother noticed an ad in a local newspaper for a correspondence school, Federal Schools (later called Art Instruction Schools). Schulz passed the talent test, completed the course, and began trying, unsuccessfully, to sell gag cartoons to magazines. (His first published drawing was of his dog, Spike, and appeared in a 1937 *Ripley's Believe It or Not!* installment.)

After World War II had ended and Schulz was discharged from the army, he started submitting gag cartoons to the various magazines of the time; his first breakthrough, however, came when an editor at *Timeless Topix* hired him to letter adventure comics. Soon after that, he was hired by his alma mater, Art Instruction, to correct student lessons returned by mail.

Between 1948 and 1950, he succeeded in selling seventeen cartoons to the *Saturday Evening Post* — as well as, to the local *St. Paul Pioneer Press*, a weekly comic feature called *Li'l Folks*. It ran in the women's section and paid ten dollars a week. After writing and drawing the feature for two years, Schulz asked for a better location in the paper or for daily exposure, as well as a raise. When he was turned down on all three counts, he quit.

He started submitting strips to the newspaper syndicates. In the spring of 1950, he received a letter from the United Feature Syndicate, announcing its interest in his submission, *Li'l Folks*. Schulz boarded a train in June for New York City; more interested in doing a strip than a panel, he also brought along the first installments of what would become *Peanuts* — and that was what sold. (The title, which Schulz loathed to his dying day, was imposed by the syndicate). The first *Peanuts* daily appeared October 2, 1950; the first Sunday, January 6, 1952.

Prior to *Peanuts*, the province of the comics page had been that of gags, social and political observation, domestic comedy, soap opera, and various adventure genres. Although *Peanuts* changed, or evolved, during the fifty years Schulz wrote and drew it, it remained, as it began, an anomaly on the comics page — a comic strip about the interior crises of the cartoonist himself. After a painful divorce in 1973 from which he had not yet recovered, Schulz told a reporter, "Strangely, I've drawn better cartoons in the last six months — or as good as I've ever drawn. I don't know how the human mind works." Surely, it was this kind of humility in the face of profoundly irreducible human questions that makes *Peanuts* as universally moving as it is.

Diagnosed with cancer, Schulz retired from *Peanuts* at the end of 1999. He died on February 12, 2000, the day before his last strip was published (and two days before Valentine's Day) — having completed 17,897 daily and Sunday strips, each and every one fully written, drawn, and lettered entirely by his own hand — an unmatched achievement in comics.

—Gary Groth

ART! ART! ART! ART! ART!
WHAM
WHAM
WHAM
WHAM
WHAM